Roadtrippers

Route 66
Chicago to Santa Monica

GREAT AMERICAN ROAD TRIPS

Roadtrippers Route 66: Chicago to Santa Monica

First edition, second printing 2022
Copyright © 2021 by Roadtrippers LLC

Editor: Kate Johnson
Contributors: Tatiana Parent, Sanna Boman, Alexandra Charitan, Stephanie
    Puglisi, Melissa Haskin, and Tag Christof
Book design: Fallon Venable and Travis Bryant
Cover design, maps, and chapter openers: Scott McGrew
Interior photos: Tatiana Parent, unless noted on page or on page 296
Proofreader: Rebecca Henderson
Indexer: Rich Carlson

Library of Congress Cataloging-in-Publication Data

Title: Roadtrippers Route 66: Chicago to Santa Monica.
Description: First edition. | Birmingham, AL : Roadtrippers, an imprint of
    AdventureKEEN, [2021]
Identifiers: LCCN 2020031407 (print) | LCCN 2020031408 (ebook) | ISBN
    9781649010001 (pbk.) | ISBN 1649010001 (pbk.) | ISBN 9781649010018
    (ebook)
Subjects: LCSH: Automobile travel--United States Highway 66--Guidebooks.
    | United States Highway 66--Guidebooks
Classification: LCC GV1024 .R716 2021 (pbk.) | LCC GV1024 (ebook)
    | DDC 917.8--dc23
LC record available at lccn.loc.gov/2020031407
LC ebook record available at lccn.loc.gov/2020031408

Published by Roadtrippers
An imprint of AdventureKEEN
2204 First Ave. S., Ste. 102
Birmingham, AL 35233
800-678-7006, fax 877-374-9016

Visit adventurewithkeen.com for a complete listing of our books and for ordering information. Contact us at our website, at facebook.com/adventurekeen, or
at twitter.com/adventurekeen with questions or comments.

Front cover photos: Arizona Road: © Konoplytska/Shutterstock; '57 Chevy Bel Air:
© Stan Rohrer/Alamy; sign: © StockPhotoAstur/Alamy; Gemini Giant: © David
Vilaplana/Alamy
Back cover photo: Big Texan Steak Ranch: © Bob Pardue–Southwest/Alamy

Manufactured in China
Distributed by Publishers Group West

SAFETY NOTICE Although Roadtrippers and the authors have made every
attempt to ensure that the information in this book is accurate at press time, they
are not responsible for any loss, damage, injury, or inconvenience that may occur
to anyone while using this book. You are responsible for your own safety and
health while traveling. Always check local conditions, know your limitations,
and consult a map. *Note:* As this book went to press, the coronavirus pandemic
was still affecting the operations of many local businesses. If you plan to visit
those listed in this book, consider calling ahead of time or checking their websites
for current closures and hours of operation.

Table of contents

LEG 2: St. Louis to Tulsa 76

LEG 3: Tulsa to Amarillo 114

LEG 4: Amarillo to Albuquerque 158

LEG 5: Albuquerque to Flagstaff 206

LEG 6: Flagstaff to Santa Monica 244

Welcome to Roadtrippers.

We're so glad you're here.

What is Roadtrippers?

Roadtrippers is a road trip planner, a digital magazine, an app, and a travel resource—but above all else, we're a group of individuals with a shared love for the road. We live in different cities, come from different backgrounds, and drive different types of vehicles, but we all want to help you plan the best road trip possible.

Whether you're a motorcyclist looking for the most scenic roads, a family exploring the country's national parks in an RV, a recent graduate driving cross-country to relocate after college, or someone just looking for a fun weekend adventure, we've got you covered.

With the Roadtrippers Plus app, you can create a trip from point A to point B, and we'll give you suggestions on what to see and do along the route. You can also collaborate with friends, get live traffic updates, and receive exclusive offers and discounts. Our database includes millions of places, and we firmly believe that you're never more than 5 minutes from something amazing. Prove us wrong!

Need some inspiration before hitting the road? Check out *Roadtrippers Magazine* for stories about the most interesting people and places out there. We've covered everything from whimsical roadside attractions to abandoned theme parks to museums operated by religious cults.

Roadtrippers is the only trip-planning tool designed to make your trip longer.

BELOW Venice Canal Historic District (page 293)
wonderlustpicstravel/Shutterstock

Take that detour. We promise it'll be worth it.

Enhance your guidebook with the Roadtrippers Plus app

Learn more about Roadtrippers Plus:
rt.guide/HHAP

Why Roadtrippers Plus?

The #1 road trip planning app just got way better. With Roadtrippers Plus, you can build epically long trips, collaborate with friends, and get exclusive deals.

The absolute best road trip planning solution. Everything you'd expect from the best in travel tech with access to more advanced features. It's the ultimate companion for the most epic road trip.

Plan Longer Trips	**New Map Styles**
No Ads	**Live Traffic**
Offline Maps	**Amazing Deals**
Collaboration	**Roadtrippers Reviews**

With Roadtrippers Plus, we're able to improve upon our already powerful product and offer cool new features and exclusive content to you, the road trip essentialist. Our free version will always be, well, **free.**

Get the premiere RV road trip app: Togo RV

Learn more about Togo RV:
rt.guide/CZHS

Togo RV is the ultimate app to keep RV owners organized, inspired, and on the move. Transform time spent on vehicle maintenance and trip preparations into time spent enjoying your RV and hitting the open road!

Navigate with directions specific to your RV

Use our premade checklists

Find nearby RV service centers

Discover what's around you

Connect with mobile RV repair

Get recall alerts for your RV

Planning a road trip

Read more road trip planning tips:
rt.guide/ZSTN

If you're jonesing to plan an epic road trip adventure but don't know where to start, the experts at Road-trippers have you covered. Here's everything you need to plan the perfect road trip.

STEP 1: Decide the basics

Figure out what you most want to see. Forget about what others recommend you *should* see, and decide what you *want* to see, whether it's mountains, beaches, deserts, farm country, national parks, cityscapes, or a little bit of everything.

Consider a theme. Some travelers like to pick a theme to tie a road trip together. Themes can inspire ideas and help you focus on the itinerary. Need some inspiration? Try spring training, historical sites, famous filming locations, outdoor adventures, architecture, theme parks, or culinary travel.

Embrace your roadtripping style. There is no one-size-fits-all itinerary for your dream road trip. Embracing the freedom of the open road and your own personal

ABOVE Rainbow Bridge in Baxter Springs, Kansas (page 103)
Chris Higgins Photography/Shutterstock

traveling style allows you to savor the experience. If it's all about getting to the destination and making only necessary pit stops, that's cool. If it's all about the journey, take shorter drives with lots of planned and unplanned stops. Do guided tours with new people rock your world, or do you like to take the reins and chart your own course? Trust your own traveling style and embrace what works for you.

Set a budget. Having a budget in mind will help steer you in the right direction. If your wallet is light, road trips offer many ways to control costs and still have fun, from staying in classic motels and eating at cheaper road-food joints to charting shorter routes to save on gas. Want to blow your bonus in style? Splurge on higher-end accommodations, fancy eateries, and private tours.

STEP 2: Create an itinerary

The Roadtrippers app and website make the planning process easy. While you're routing out your trip, explore the Roadtrippers map to get inspired. The Extraordinary Places icons highlight our favorite stops, and *Roadtrippers Magazine* offers up even more road trip inspiration. You can choose up to seven waypoints on the free version of the app, or more with Roadtrippers Plus. Layer in interesting things to see and do along your route, and sort by categories such as accommodations, entertainment, gas stations, restaurants, and more. Roadtrippers calculates the best route for you, including time and distance between stops and your destination. It will also calculate the approximate cost of gasoline for the whole journey.

As you get more experienced with roadtripping, you can find more tools with Roadtrippers Plus, which helps you plan longer trips and offers turn-by-turn directions.

STEP 3: Bypass potential roadblocks with a little planning

Some travelers glorify winging it, but no planning at all can lead to epic misadventures. Here are a few scenarios where you might want to plan ahead so your road trip doesn't come to a screeching halt.

Lodging: Book at least some of your lodging in advance, especially if it's peak tourist season or you're traveling with a pet, as your options may be scarce. If you'd still like to leave it all up to serendipity, look for off-the-beaten-path motels and campgrounds that are less likely to fill up in advance.

Hours of operation: Before you go, check the hours, days, and seasons of operation for places you want to see, since third-party apps and articles can easily become out of date.

Food and drink: If you're hungry for something local, don't settle for the lone fast-food restaurant you spotted after hours of driving. Using the Food & Drink category or search tool on the Roadtrippers app can help you find everything from celebrity eateries to burger joints and diners.

Routes: The Roadtrippers app will help you plan the basics while leaving plenty of room for kismet.

STEP 4: Brush up on your local knowledge

If the idea of living like a local for the day is appealing, bide your time between planning a road trip and hitting the road by following regional accounts and hashtags on social media. Read fiction and nonfiction books about the region or route. Watch movies and YouTube videos.

Check out *Roadtrippers Magazine* articles for great stories about famous (and infamous) points of interest.

If that's too much planning for your style, you can get advice while on the road by asking the proprietors of campgrounds, hotels, and Airbnbs along the way for their best local intel.

STEP 5: Stay flexible, always

Have a plan to make sure your road trip is everything you want it to be, but leave space for unexpected opportunities. Inexperienced travelers often get too ambitious with their first itinerary, finding themselves drained and stressed when things don't go exactly according to plan. A great roadtripper is always willing to veer from the plan for the right reason. A great way to find that balance is to download the Roadtrippers app and take it with you, so you can have all the information you need at your fingertips—from verifying driving distances between planned stops to getting ideas for charting a completely new course.

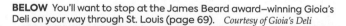

BELOW You'll want to stop at the James Beard award–winning Gioia's Deli on your way through St. Louis (page 69). *Courtesy of Gioia's Deli*

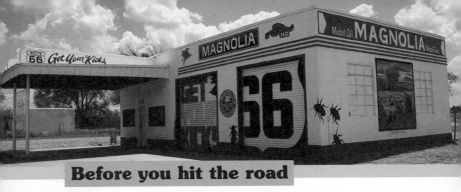

Before you hit the road

Read more about getting ready to hit the road:
rt.guide/GNXS

Preparing your home

When you're leaving for a road trip, the last thing you need is the sudden suspicion that you left the stove on or forgot to throw out that carton of leftover lo mein.

Deep-cleaning your home close to departure day will help keep you organized. Take out all the garbage, ditch any perishable food, and organize the things you've been putting off, like that stack of unopened mail. It's always kind of a bummer when a fun road trip comes to an end, but it's even more of a bummer if you're coming home to a bunch of chores.

Make a list of the things that need to be taken care of while you're gone. Ask a neighbor or friend to get your mail and water your plants, or have your mail put on hold to be picked up at the post office when you're back.

If your pet isn't coming with you, find someone to care for it. Plan a vet appointment well in advance of your trip to confirm your furry friends are all set for a little vacation—especially if they're going to a kennel.

ABOVE Magnolia gas station in Tucumcari, New Mexico (page 174)

Bringing a furry companion with you? There are lots of places that pets can't go, like certain hotels and national parks. Bringing a pet on a road trip can be a lot of fun, but you'll need to research your destinations and their pet policies. BringFido.com is a popular website for finding dog-friendly hotels, restaurants, parks, and more.

Securing your home

Installing a home security system before you leave can offer peace of mind. But there are cheaper options for keeping your home safe and sound. Leave a light or two on (or keep them on a timer), and maintain any house services, like lawn care or pool upkeep. An outdoor sensor light is an inexpensive and generally effective deterrent to would-be snoopers and thieves. Leave a key with a neighbor you trust, just in case someone needs to get in.

Packing your vehicle

An overpacked car can quickly turn into a disorganized mess, and you're likely to forget about half the stuff you brought if it's not easy to access. With that in mind, focus on accessibility and multifunctional items.

A small overnight bag should contain everything you need after a long day of driving—think sleepwear, toiletries, and a good book.

Your car should be packed according to what you'll need first. Items specific to a destination farther down the road, or gear for weather that might occur later in your trip, should be packed beneath items you'll need regularly or right away.

PACKING FOR A ROAD TRIP

Every packing list will be different, depending on where you're going, what you're doing, and how long you'll be gone. We'll get you started with the basics.

- **Camping supplies.** Tent, sleeping bag, sleeping pad, stove, and lantern.

- **Cash.** For highway tolls, campground fees, and unexpected cash-only stops.

- **Closed-toe, active shoes.** Bring hiking boots, sneakers, or both, depending on your preferred activities.

- **Comfortable driving clothes**

- **Duffel bags or packing cubes.** Soft-sided carriers will make it easier to separate your things for different legs of the trip, and they're easy to stack and smoosh together.

- **Garbage bags.** Keep all your waste in one place.

- **First aid kit.** Adhesive bandages, aspirin, antiseptic, Dramamine for car sickness, and any other medication you might need.

- **Hands-free cell phone holder**

- **Headlamp.** Even if you're not camping, this will help you find things in your car at night.

- **Medium-warmth coat.** Functional layers are the key to comfort when roadtripping.

- **Notebook and pen.** For recommendations, journaling, games, and more.

- **Phone chargers.** At least two—one should stay in your car so you always know where it is.

- **Pillow and extra blankets**

- **Road atlas.** A seasoned roadtripper always has a current one in the car.

- **Slip-on shoes.** Camping slippers or hiking sandals are great for midnight bathroom runs or driving.

- **Sunglasses.** Bring the cheap ones; you're bound to lose a pair or two.

- **Toiletries**

- **Towel.** For the beach, showers, sitting in the grass, the dog, etc.

- **Travel mug and reusable water bottles.** You'll save money and cut down on waste.

- **Water.** It's always a good idea to have an extra gallon or two on hand.

Last-minute reminders

You can experience such a range of conditions when driving long distances, and road trip experiences can be ruined by poor planning, weather changes, navigation snafus, and too many opinions from the backseat.

You can be better prepared for the challenges and mishaps of roadtripping by knowing what you want out of your trip. You might have lots of ideas for where to stop and what to see, but pick just one or two that can't be missed, and prioritize accordingly.

Weather can be tricky to track along a route, especially if you're driving long distances in one day. But you definitely want to know if a snowstorm is brewing at mile 300 of your 600-mile day. Download an app like WeatherBUG, which lets you to track more than one location at once.

For entertainment, download playlists for offline use before you begin your trip. Ask for recommendations for music, podcasts, and audiobooks to keep things fresh on those less interesting stretches of flat highway.

Give yourself time to embrace the unexpected. You can't possibly anticipate everything the road has in store for you—and that's part of the fun.

BELOW Palo Duro Canyon State Park in Canyon, Texas (page 147)

Getting your car road-trip ready

 Read more about getting your car ready for a road trip: **rt.guide/TTNW**

Even after you have the route planned and you know the major attractions you want to hit, there are still a few more logistics you need to consider. Specifically, you need to make sure your vehicle is up to the task.

In terms of the best car for a road trip, there's no universal solution, but there are some features to consider depending on your situation. If it's just you, then the smaller the better. You want something that can hold all of your gear, of course, but generally speaking, smaller vehicles get better gas mileage. A separate trunk is a bonus because it gives you more-secure storage. At the same time, if you think you might car camp from time to time, then a hatchback or wagon might be a better option.

For most people, a compact SUV is likely the best balance. If you know you'll be going down some rough roads, look into one that has four-wheel drive or all-wheel drive. That opens up a ton of possibilities for things to see and places to camp, and it should strike a nice balance between storage space, gas mileage, and mobility.

Your car's age isn't nearly as important as the question "How is it running?" Road trips put a lot of long,

ABOVE Cadillac Ranch in Amarillo, Texas (page 153)
Courtesy of Amarillo CVC

ABOVE Ariston Cafe in Litchfield, Illinois (page 57)

hard hours on all of your car's systems. Try to be as impartial as you can be when evaluating it. Have you been hearing sounds of grinding or rubbing? That can develop into a major problem when you're driving hundreds of miles at a time. Also consider the kind of terrain you're hoping to tackle. Are you wanting to get off the grid? If your car's suspension is getting old and tired, you may want to look into another solution. The best thing to do is take your car to a professional mechanic you trust and have them do a full inspection. If your car isn't up to it, don't despair: You might consider a rental (see sidebar on opposite page).

When preparing your vehicle for a trip, it's always good to bring a first aid kit and road flares. Consider keeping some extra nonperishable food and water in your vehicle just in case you get stranded for a bit. You'll also want flashlights, extra batteries, and an external USB charger to keep your gadgets running. Some spare warm, waterproof clothing and a blanket could also save your life in a pinch.

THE PROS AND CONS OF RENTING A CAR FOR YOUR ROAD TRIP

Pros:

- You can get a newer vehicle that runs better, gets better mileage, and has better features.
- You can get a vehicle specific to your task. If you want to off-road, you can get a four-wheel-drive vehicle. Or if you'll be traveling with a bunch of people, maybe a passenger van is the way to go.
- Generally speaking, if something goes wrong, rentals offer roadside assistance, and you won't be left footing the bill for mechanical problems.
- You won't be adding wear and tear to your daily driver.

Cons:

- The biggest con is the cost. Rentals typically aren't cheap, though you may be able to get a better deal from companies that rent older vehicles or vehicles with cosmetic issues.
- You can't modify the vehicle for your needs.
- Some rental companies will limit the places you can go and the types of roads you can go on.
- Any physical damage the car sustains may cost you, unless you pay for additional insurance.

Tips for traveling
Route 66 by motorcycle

 Read more about roadtripping by motorcycle:
rt.guide/CRAM

There's arguably no better way to travel across the United States than to do it *Easy Rider* style: by motorcycle. Being on two wheels means a much more up-close connection to your surroundings than what the confines of a car can offer. But it also comes with its unique challenges. Here are some things to keep in mind as you prepare for your epic adventure.

1. Choose the right bike

Whether you're riding your own trusty steed or renting one for the trip, it's important to make sure you have the correct motorcycle for your height and weight as well as the type of riding you're planning on doing. Can you sit comfortably in the same position for hours on end? Does the bike have enough built-in storage or room for added luggage? Are you planning on doing any off-roading or will you be sticking to paved roads? The answers to these questions should help you narrow down whether you need a touring bike, a cruiser, an adventure bike, or something completely different.

2. Pack for all-weather travel

Riding a motorcycle means being completely exposed to the elements. You'll feel every wind gust, rain drop, or temperature change in a way that someone in a car never will. Route 66 passes through eight states with widely varying climates. Depending on when you travel, you may need to prepare for everything from snow to rainstorms to desert heat. Pack layers—that way you can easily bulk up or strip down as needed along the route. A rain suit, waterproof gloves, and boot covers will be lifesavers in the event of heavy rain. And if you're traveling during the winter months, consider investing in some heated gear.

3. Take frequent breaks

Spending long hours on a motorcycle tends to make everything hurt at the end of the day. One way to help combat the worst saddle sores is to take frequent breaks. Carry plenty of water and snacks to stave off dehydration or blood sugar drops. It's tempting to just gas up and keep going, but make a habit out of getting off the bike to stretch and have a snack every time you come to a stop. It will make the entire trip that much more enjoyable.

4. Bring tools

The most reliable thing about motorcycles is their unre-liability. It's wise to hope for the best while preparing for the worst. Long-haul road trips require continuous maintenance—tires wear out, parts rattle loose, and oil may need to be refilled or replaced. It's a good idea to carry a basic tool kit for roadside fixes. Make sure you bring the correct tools for your bike (know whether it's metric or imperial). Other items that can come in handy in a pinch are zip ties, extra bungee cords, and electrical tape.

Tips for international travelers

 Find information for international
roadtrippers: **rt.guide/XYYL**

Passports and visas

When traveling to the United States, you're typically
required to have a passport that is valid for six months
beyond your intended stay. However, if your home
country is among 125 nations exempt from this rule,
your passport needs to be valid only for the time of
your visit. Check the U.S. Customs and Border Protec-
tion website (cbp.gov) for a current list.

Generally, you must obtain a nonimmigrant visa, but
if your home country is part of the Visa Waiver Program,
you can travel without a visa. However, you still need
prior approval through the Electronic System for Travel
Authorization (ESTA). For details, consult the U.S.
Department of State website (travel.state.gov/content
/travel/en/us-visas/tourism-visit/visitor.html).

Driver's license requirements

Bring your valid driver's license from your own country. In addition, some states and rental companies
require an International Driving Permit (IDP), which
you can obtain from your motor vehicle department.

And remember, you'll be driving on the right-hand
side of the road.

Car rental

Most car rental companies require that the driver be at
least 20 or 21 years old. However, drivers younger than
25 may be charged an additional surcharge.

The cost depends on several factors: the size of the car, rental location, trip length, and time of year. You'll most likely pay more for a one-way rental.

Major car rental companies include Avis, Alamo, Budget, Dollar, Enterprise, Hertz, National, Sixt, and Thrifty.

RV rental

A recreational vehicle (RV) is a popular choice for road trips. While you'll save money on hotel expenses and dining out, you'll pay more for fuel and the rental itself. In the end, your overall costs are likely to be about the same. The real advantages? You need to unpack only once, and you'll be closer to nature.

The minimum age to rent an RV is 21 or 25 years old, depending on the rental company and the state where you're renting. Again, extra fees may apply for young drivers. You don't need a special license to drive an RV.

For international visitors, we recommend a Class B (think camper van) or Class C RV. The average gas mileage for a Class B is 18 to 25 miles per gallon (about 7 to 10 kilometers per liter); for a Class C, it's 14 to 18 miles per gallon (about 6 to 7 kilometers per liter).

Some nationwide rental companies include Cruise America, El Monte RV, and Road Bear RV. You also can rent a privately owned RV through peer-to-peer rental platforms. Or look for an independent RV dealer in your departure city.

Vehicle insurance

Check to see if your personal car insurance, credit card insurance, or traveler's insurance will cover your vehicle rental. If not, you'll be given the option to purchase coverage from the rental company.

Tolls

A few major highways are toll roads. Some toll collectors accept credit cards; others don't. Make sure to have cash on hand.

Fuel

Most gas stations will allow you to pay by credit card at the pump, but this option is available only if you have a U.S.-issued credit card with a zip code. Instead, plan to pay inside before you pump. You can pump your own gas in every state except New Jersey and Oregon.

Types of accommodations

If you're driving:
Bed-and-breakfast inns: Typically large homes that have been converted into inns, B&Bs have free breakfast.

Hostels: You're more likely to find hostels in large cities. Make sure to note whether the rooms and bathrooms are shared with other guests.

Hotels: Hotels can vary from affordable chain brands to five-star luxury splurges. Several chains include a complimentary breakfast in your stay.

Motels: These affordable, roadside accommodations have rooms with outside-facing doors and are common along Route 66.

Privately owned rooms, apartments, or homes: Look for short-term rentals on websites like Airbnb, FlipKey, HomeAway, Vacasa, and VRBO.

If you're RVing:
State parks: These affordable campgrounds typically offer hookups for water and sometimes electricity but rarely sewage. Tent sites and cabins may be available.

National parks: Similar to state parks, national park campgrounds are in high demand and should be reserved six to nine months in advance.

Commercial campgrounds: Privately owned campgrounds normally offer full hookups, including water, electricity, sewage, and cable television. They may have additional amenities like kids' programs, camp stores, and swimming pools.

Money

Credit cards are widely accepted.

If you need cash, ATMs can be found at banks, shopping malls, grocery stores, convenience stores, and gas stations. Check with your local bank to ensure that your debit or credit card will work in the United States. Also, ask about fees charged for withdrawing money.

You can exchange money at airport kiosks and at some banks.

Tipping

At sit-down restaurants and bars, it's customary to tip your waiter 15 to 20 percent of the pretax cost of your meal or drinks. You don't tip at fast-food restaurants. Tipping is optional at coffee houses and food carts.

Cell phones

Because most international phones use GSM technology, you'll want to purchase a U.S.-based SIM card from either a T-Mobile or AT&T store; prepaid SIM cards aren't always available at U.S. airports. If your road trip will take you through rural areas, you're better off with AT&T's wider coverage. Make sure your phone is unlocked, and activate the SIM card while you're still in the store to avoid any problems.

Alternatively, you could use your home-based SIM card and pay the often-expensive international roaming fees. Check with your provider for details.

For emergencies (police, fire, ambulance), dial 911.

Internet access

Nearly every hotel will offer complimentary WiFi. You'll also find free internet access at most cafés. Some cities offer free WiFi in public spaces.

Choosing your route

Will you go from Chicago to Los Angeles, or vice versa? Travelers often choose the east-to-west direction, as that's the route originally taken by families escaping the Dust Bowl in the 1920s. Either way, you'll find ample international flights in and out of Chicago O'Hare International Airport (ORD) and Los Angeles International Airport (LAX).

Determining the duration of your trip

Typically, travelers will plan no less than two weeks for the entire Mother Road road trip. In that amount of time, you'll be able to visit the major sites. But if you want to savor the entire experience—strolling historic downtowns, sipping a root beer float at a soda fountain, and sleeping at a retro motel with a blinking neon sign—you could spend up to a month or longer.

An introduction to Route 66

To drive Route 66 in its entirety is to feel the American landscape in high fidelity, just as a record player's needle finds the scratches on a well-loved album. It is one of the final places to experience the U.S. as an endless frontier, a snapshot of an era of unprecedented change and progress. And in a society that always seems so focused on the next big thing, the Mother Road's enduring appeal is its roadside treasures and stories of human hope.

Although it existed as a unified, legally codified road only for 59 years—from 1926 until 1985, when the interstate system officially superseded it—Route 66 became a great symbolic trailway of human civilization. It will live forever as a route whose traffic reshaped the world of its time, transporting generations of adventurers, migrants, grifters, and dreamers toward untold opportunities.

Route 66 gave rise to new towns, new industries, and a new vernacular architecture. A great deal of it was lost when most cross-country travel migrated to the interstates, but today a thriving community of people who live along the road—travelers, well-wishers, and preservationists—share news and stories, raise money to protect landmarks, maintain museums, and otherwise work hard to protect its legacy. The route's future, thanks to roadtrippers like you, looks bright.

ABOVE Chicago skyline (page 34)
JamesAndrews1/Shutterstock

The Mother Road has been firmly embedded in the American mythos for decades. In the 1940s, Bobby Troup pounded out "(Get Your Kicks On) Route 66," a catchy and enduring standard that has been covered by dozens of artists, from Nat King Cole to The Cramps. In the 1960s, CBS notched a major hit with *Route 66,* a series whose plot mostly amounted to two handsome guys rambling around the country in a Corvette roadster. Very few of the show's episodes were actually set in towns anywhere near the road it was named for, making it clear that Route 66 had already become shorthand for the adventuresome American spirit, and for the open road itself. And since the Mother Road disappeared from official maps and its signage was removed in 1985, its mystique has only grown.

Route 66's most powerful symbols—the buzzing neon motel sign, the diner with its tar-black coffee and surly but endearing waitresses, the kitschy tourist trap—have all become part of the basic vocabulary of the American road in literature, film, and art. From Steinbeck to Disney's *Cars,* it seems that every great road story is somehow connected to Route 66. We're no exception: For Roadtrippers, this iconic route is foundational for our love of road trips and how we tell stories.

Throughout the journey from Chicago to Santa Monica, you'll discover sections where the original route diverges, seemingly shooting off in two directions and yet nowhere at once. It is a prime lesson in the art of the road trip: A sudden change in direction, an abrupt end to the pavement, and a few wrong turns are all welcome parts of the adventure rather than an inconvenience.

The road advances gently from its easternmost beginning under the gilded towers of Chicago's Michigan Avenue through the flat, fertile farmlands of Illinois and Missouri. The west seems to begin in earnest somewhere around the big Blue Whale of Catoosa in Oklahoma, and has totally set in by the time you reach Cadillac Ranch and the gut-busting portions at Amarillo's Big Texan Steak Ranch. And just before you reach the sparkling Pacific, there is still a treasure trove of roadside gems along the route just east of Los Angeles: the western-most remaining Wigwam Motel, the Magic Lamp Inn with vinyl booths and a copper-hooded fire pit, and the resplendent Streamline Moderne racetrack at Santa Anita, among at least a dozen others.

Route 66 is the quintessential embodiment of the road and all its greatest promises: freedom and seren-dipity, kitsch and living history, and a case study of the very particular way Americans have moved and multi-plied. You can certainly travel eastward on Route 66 (in fact, we highly recommend it), but there's no denying the symbolic strength of at least one westward journey along its patchwork of asphalt. Hop in!

Best time to travel

The best time to drive Route 66 is from late April to early October. Be prepared for remnants of ice and snow during the early spring and thunderstorms in late spring and early summer. During July and August—peak travel months—expect sometimes-swel-tering temperatures, overcrowded attractions, and higher rates for lodging.

Come late October and into November, you might see snowfall on parts of the route. Winter is considered the off-season, and some places may be closed until spring, so it's always best to call ahead if you're ven-turing out onto Route 66 between late November and early April. Whatever time you travel, expect variations in climate, as you'll be traversing many different states and terrains.

How to use this guide

 Find up-to-date digital content for this Route
66 guide: **rt.guide/route66**

This book has everything you need to plan an epic
Route 66 roadtripping adventure, with an awesome
digital bonus. At rt.guide/route66 you will find interactive trip guides and maps that include every single
roadside attraction, museum, photo op, and restaurant
listed in this book. Use our online trip planner to cus-
tomize the route, adding or deleting waypoints to create
a personalized plan. Once you hit the road, use the
Roadtrippers app to navigate and discover even more
interesting stops along the way.

Westbound versus eastbound travel

Use this guidebook for either westbound (Chicago to
Santa Monica) or eastbound (Santa Monica to Chicago)
travel along Route 66. For simplicity, the book is organized from east to west, as that's the most popular way
to experience the route. Should you venture from California to Illinois, just read this book in reverse, starting
with leg 6.

SIDEBAR CATEGORIES

 Route highlights: There's a lot to see on the Mother Road. We'll give you a selection of must-see places at the beginning of every route section.

 Playlists: For each leg of the trip, we've curated some great tunes for your listening pleasure. Each playlist corresponds with where you'll be and provides a cool reflection of each area's unique culture.

 Fun random factoids: Learn some fun facts about the places you'll be passing through.

 Weirdville: This is where you'll learn more about cryptids, urban legends, and UFOs. We'll also include some ghost guides for the haunted hotels you can stay in along the road.

 Spotlight: These are expanded descriptions of unique places along the route that will provide a deeper understanding of iconic spots.

 Detours: Interesting places that are slightly off the main route, but where we think it's worth going the extra mile. We'll also suggest fun side trips if you've got extra time.

 48-Hour guides: Some of our favorite things to do if you have a little extra time to spend in certain cities.

 URLs: Find expanded information, fascinating magazine stories, and digital trip guides.

CLASSIC ROAD TRIP MOVIE INSPIRATION

Bagdad Cafe (1987) is based on an actual restaurant that was located on Route 66 until it was abandoned. The film is a love letter to those service stations, cafés, and motels that brought together road-weary travelers.

Disney Pixar's *Cars* (2006) is the ultimate Route 66 road trip movie. It follows Lightning McQueen, a race car who disappears in the town of Radiator Springs. The town is reflective of places such as Galena, Kansas; Shamrock, Texas; Holbrook, Arizona; and Tucumcari, New Mexico.

Easy Rider (1969) is the story of two biker hippies who take a road trip and reflect on America.

Little Miss Sunshine (2006) follows a dysfunctional and quirky family of six who are roadtripping to a beauty pageant in a 1971 Volkswagen bus.

Thelma and Louise (1991) is about two best friends who roadtrip from Arkansas to Arizona and seriously take their trip too far.

Inspired to start planning your epic Route 66 road trip?

Get ready to head to the Windy City, where your first leg of the adventure begins.

Cadillac Ranch
Amarillo, TX

07

**Elmer's Bottle
Tree Ranch**
Oro Grande, CA

10

Flagstaff
Arizona

09

08

11

SANTA MONICA
66
End of the Trail

Santa Monica
California

Albuquerque
New Mexico

Chicago
Illinois

St. Louis
Missouri

Amarillo
Texas

01

02

03

04

05

06

**World's Largest
Catsup Bottle**
Collinsville, IL

Tulsa
Oklahoma

Blue Whale of Catoosa
Catoosa, OK

Leg 1: Chicago to St. Louis

316 Miles

Find a complete Online Trip Guide for leg 1:

rt.guide/AXKA

Chicago
Illinois

01

02

Standard Oil Station
Odell, IL

03

Gemini Giant
Wilmington, IL

**Cozy Dog
Drive-In**
Springfield, IL

04

05

06

**World's Largest
Catsup Bottle**
Collinsville, IL

St. Louis
Missouri

Leg 1: Chicago to St. Louis

Route highlights

01 Chicago

Gemini Giant **02**

03 Standard Oil Station

Cozy Dog Drive In **04**

05 World's Largest Catsup Bottle

St. Louis **06**

Featured campgrounds

Indiana Dunes State Park
1600 N. County Road 25 E., Chesterton, IN

If you're planning on starting your Route 66 adventure in Chicago, this is the perfect campground for tenting, RVing, or cabin camping. The South Shore Line offers rail service directly from the state park to downtown Chicago.

St. Louis West/Historic Route 66 KOA
18475 Old US 66, Eureka, MO

This campground sits right on historic Route 66 and offers a heated pool, a playground, a jump pillow, and gem mining. Plus, it's located less than a mile from Six Flags.

Featured accommodation

The Pasfield House Inn
525 S. Pasfield St., Springfield, IL

This 1896 mansion has been converted into a bed-and-breakfast. It's located close to all the major attractions in Springfield. For more on The Pasfield House Inn, see page 56.

Playlist
Listen here: rt.guide/DLNT

Songs to get you in the mood while on the road . . .

1. "Route 66," Chuck Berry
2. "Illinois," Brett Eldredge
3. "Chicago," Sufjan Stevens
4. "My Kind of Town," Frank Sinatra
5. "Lake Shore Drive," Aliotta Haynes Jeremiah
6. "Illinois," The Everly Brothers
7. "Illinois Blues," Skip James
8. "Chicago Breakdown," Big Maceo
9. "Have a Good Time," Big Walter Horton
10. "Little Boy Blue," Big Walter Horton
11. "I'm a Man," Bo Diddley
12. "Mustang Sally," Buddy Guy
13. "Going to Chicago," Fenton Robinson
14. "Highway Man Blues," Jimmy Dawkins

On the road . . .
Illinois

Chicago, Illinois, is the eastern terminus of the Mother Road—depending on which way you travel, you will either start or end your trip across from Grant Park and Lake Michigan. Over the years, various road realignments and improvements meant that the route was, and still is, ever-evolving. Today many of these iterations still exist in some capacity throughout the Land of Lincoln. After leaving the Windy City, the road takes you southwest through rural Midwestern towns full of classic motel neon, vintage filling stations, roadside giants, and historic bridges until you hit the Mississippi River and East St. Louis.

Illinois is known as the Land of Lincoln because the tall guy—and eventual president—spent most of his adult life in the state. So prepare to see plenty of Honest Abe–inspired roadside wonders on this stretch.

The stretch of Route 66 from Chicago to St. Louis is home to aluminum-and-chrome diners; historic, family-owned cafes; bizarre attractions; and other reminders of the route's charming past. You'll also see plenty of cornfields and flat prairie land between the bustling cities and sleepy towns along this first leg.

There are nearly 300 miles of Route 66 in Illinois. The state is also home to many of the country's most famous Muffler Men, those fiberglass titans of retro roadside kitsch (see Detour, page 46). A lot of the old route has been gobbled up by modern highways, in particular I-55, but there's still plenty of neon, fiberglass, and chrome to keep any roadtripper happy. Traditionally, travelers begin their journey southwest near the shores of Lake Michigan, not spending too much time in Chicago. After all, the Mother Road is calling.

On the road . . .
Chicago

Start your epic journey at the route's original 1937 terminus at Lake Shore Drive and East Jackson Drive in downtown Chicago. Don't miss the ROUTE 66 STARTS HERE sign at the corner of South Michigan Avenue and East Adams Street. The sign (along with a handful of replica signs on the same block) is located in a busy section, so you may need to find parking elsewhere and walk to the sign for a photo.

Lou Mitchell's Restaurant & Bakery
565 W. Jackson Blvd., Chicago, IL

Lou Mitchell's is the perfect place to get breakfast and a cup of the "world's finest coffee" before you leave the Windy City. The restaurant has been serving home-cooked comfort food to travelers since 1923, predating the designation of Route 66 by three years. Before sitting down, diners are handed a freshly made donut hole and a miniature box of candy. And because one donut hole is never enough, you can order some to go.

Extra stops

Buckingham Fountain *Photo Op*
301 S. Columbus Drive, Chicago, IL

Willis Tower *Attraction*
233 S. Wacker Drive, Chicago, IL

The Berghoff *Restaurant*
17 W. Adams St., Chicago, IL

Lulu's Hot Dogs *Restaurant*
1000 S. Leavitt St., Chicago, IL

Castle Car Wash *Photo Op*
3801 W. Ogden Ave., Chicago, IL

Henry's Drive-In *Restaurant*
6031 W. Ogden Ave., Cicero, IL

Hofmann Tower *Photo Op*
3910 Barrypoint Road, Lyons, IL

Weirdville

Tinley Park Lights UFO Sighting
Date: August 21, 2004
Location: Chicago, IL

On a balmy August evening in 2004, Chicago residents reported seeing a series of red or white lights that formed a triangle shape. Several videos captured the light show, and it was even reported by local news outlets. The phenomenon occurred about 45 miles from O'Hare International Airport, but the lights moved too slowly to be a commercial plane. What makes this one of the more significant UFO sightings is that it was investigated by the Mutual UFO Network (MUFON), a nonprofit with thousands of civilian volunteers. The mysterious occurrence was also featured on the History Channel's *UFO Hunters*.

ABOVE AND BELOW Dell Rhea's Chicken Basket
Above: David Wilson/FLickr/CC BY 2.0 (creativecommons.org/licenses/by/2.0)

Dell Rhea's Chicken Basket
645 Joliet Road (Historic Route 66), Willowbrook, IL

Route 66 is renowned for its classic American cuisine. If you're not still full of donut holes (or even if you are), visit Dell Rhea's Chicken Basket, just outside Chicago, for some of the best fried chicken you'll ever taste. The roadhouse has been serving its home-cooked goodness since 1946. Even if you're not ready to eat just yet, the neon sign is a good photo op.

**Montana Charlie's
Little America Flea Market** *Shopping*
255 S. Joliet Road, Bolingbrook, IL
(open on Sundays, April–October)

Rich & Creamy *Restaurant*
920 N. Broadway St., Joliet, IL

**Joliet Area Historical Museum & Route 66
Visitors Center Gift Shop** *Attraction*
204 N. Ottawa St., Joliet, IL

Rialto Square Theatre *Photo Op*
102 N. Chicago St., Joliet, IL

Route 66 Raceway *Attraction*
500 Speedway Blvd., Joliet, IL

Gemini Giant
810 E. Baltimore St., Wilmington, IL

The Illinois stretch of Route 66 is home to several
great roadside attractions, but nothing shouts retro
kitsch louder than a massive Muffler Man. Snap a
picture with the Gemini Giant at the newly reopened
Launching Pad Drive-In in Wilmington. Named for
the Gemini space program, he's one of many similar
statues made by International Fiberglass. He stands
guard over the drive-in, which also houses a gift
shop, a restaurant, and the Mini Americana Museum.

 The resurrected Launching Pad diner serves up
hot-fudge sundaes with a side of grief counseling:
rt.guide/CJKZ

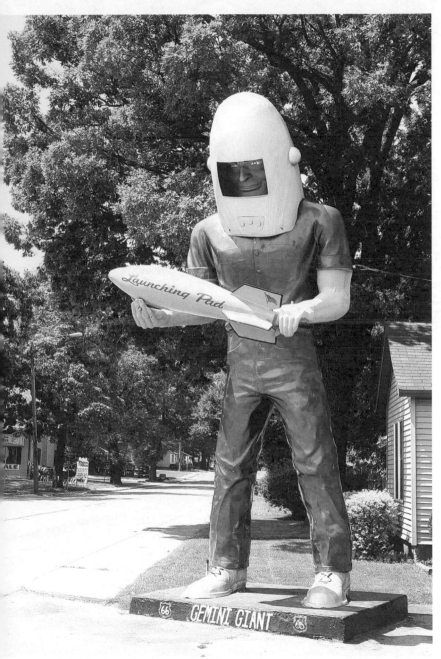

DETOUR

Meet the Muffler Men

If you took a road trip across the U.S. in the 1960s or 1970s, you probably saw more than a few Muffler Men. These tall statues often held objects like axes, swords, rifles, or tiny rocket ships. Almost all of these figures, which were created by International Fiberglass in Venice, California, had a body formed from the

ABOVE Muffler Man in Merced, California

same mold (arms out, right hand up, left hand down), but they are infinitely customizable by swapping out heads, clothes, and accessories.

These days, the term *Muffler Man* is used to describe almost any giant roadside statue advertising a business. The first Muffler Man created was a lumberjack statue produced for the Paul Bunyan Cafe off Route 66 in Flagstaff, Arizona. The statues were effective advertising tools: A Muffler Man used to cost $1,000 to $3,000 to purchase (today that number is closer to $25,000), and the 18- to 25-foot-tall figures helped grab travelers' increasingly divided attention.

At one time, thousands of International Fiberglass creations lined U.S. highways, including Sinclair Oil's dinosaurs and Phillips Petroleum's cowboys. But as freeways began to bypass the smaller routes, these giant statues fell out of favor. The gas crisis of 1973, which made production of fiberglass more expensive, dealt the final blow to International Fiberglass, which closed in 1976.

There are a few hundred Muffler Men left today, and a small group of dedicated fans have taken to restoring and caring for those that remain, including Illinois' Gemini Giant, California's Chicken Boy, New Jersey's Nitro Girl, and South Dakota's Mr. Bendo.

These repurposed Muffler Men all over the country are proof that there's value in saving forgotten roadside attractions: **rt.guide/HSRP**

Extra stops

Polk-a-Dot Drive In *Restaurant*
222 N. Front St., Braidwood, IL

Old Route 66 Family Restaurant *Restaurant*
105 S. Old Route 66, Dwight, IL

Illinois Route 66 Mining Museum
150 S. Kankakee St., Godley, IL

The Illinois Route 66 Mining Museum chronicles the significant role the coal industry played in the development of Route 66. Coal mining was the lifeblood of several small towns along the route, and this is a great place to learn how the industry affected the people and economy along what was once considered America's Main Street.

Ambler's Texaco Gas Station
W. Waupansie St., Dwight, IL

The route is dotted with old service stations, many of which have been beautifully restored and repurposed as photo ops. The first one you'll encounter is Ambler's Texaco Gas Station in Dwight. In continuous use for 66 years, from 1933 until 1999, it was one of the longest-operating gas stations on the Mother Road. Today it serves as a visitor center.

Standard Oil Gas Station
400 S. West St., Odell, IL

This station was a bustling rest stop throughout the heyday of Route 66 travel but fell into disrepair after going out of business in the late 1970s. After it was listed on the National Register of Historic Places, locals rallied to raise the funds and restore the location to its former glory.

Route 66 Association Hall of Fame and Museum
110 W. Howard St., Pontiac, IL

The Route 66 Association Hall of Fame and Museum is full of fascinating, family-friendly exhibits, and the staff's love of the route is infectious. Don't miss the wall art and wishing well in the museum's backyard.

OPPOSITE AND ABOVE Ambler's Texaco Gas Station

Old Log Cabin *Restaurant*
18700 Historic US 66, Pontiac, IL

International Walldog Mural & Sign Art Exhibit *Attraction*
110 W. Howard St., Pontiac, IL 61764

Pontiac-Oakland Automobile Museum *Attraction*
205 N. Mill St., Pontiac, IL

Ryburn Place (Sprague's Super Service) *Photo Op*
305 Pine St., Normal, IL

Cruisin' with Lincoln on 66 *Attraction*
200 N. Main St., Bloomington, IL

Funks Grove Pure Maple Sirup
5257 Historic US 66, Shirley, IL

For travelers with a sweet tooth, Funks Grove Pure Maple Sirup in Shirley is a must-see (and must-taste). Funks Grove produces more than 2,000 gallons of maple syrup—or sirup—per year using old-fashioned sap-gathering techniques. The finished product comes in beautifully designed bottles.

On the road...
Atlanta

Next up is the adorable town of Atlanta (yes, Illinois has one, too). This charming place is full of classic Route 66 attractions. Visit the town's octagonal library, built in 1908. The 40-foot-tall clock tower next door is still wound by hand every eight days.

ABOVE Clock tower in Atlanta, Illinois
Henryk Sadura/Shutterstock

ABOVE Downtown Atlanta, Illinois

Route 66 Arcade Museum
108 SW Arch St., Atlanta, IL

Atlanta is also home to the Route 66 Arcade Museum, a fantastic hidden gem. It features a collection of vintage arcade machines (made from 1934 to 1982) that you can still play for just a quarter.

Bunyon with a Hot Dog
110 SW Arch St., Atlanta, IL

Atlanta is also where you'll find the iconic 19-foot-tall Paul Bunyon Muffler Man holding a hot dog, one of the most famous statues along Route 66. He's perpetually standing guard just across from The Palms Grill Cafe. In 1965, H. A. Stephens purchased a Paul Bunyan Muffler Man, swapped its original ax for a hotdog, and placed it in front of his restaurant in Cicero, Illinois. Stephens purposely misspelled the name of his business, Bunyon's, to avoid a trademark conflict with the Paul Bunyan Cafe, site of the original statue, in Flagstaff, Arizona. A legend was born, and over the years the Bunyon statue, now on loan to Atlanta, became a Route 66 landmark.

Lincoln Watermelon Monument
101 N. Chicago St., Lincoln, IL

After visiting Paul Bunyan and his hot dog, head over to the town of Lincoln to check out one of its more bizarre presidential monuments—a statue of a 2-foot-long watermelon. In 1853, before he was president, Abraham Lincoln visited the town during its naming celebration. He grabbed a watermelon from a nearby stand, juiced it, and then gave a speech. More than 100 years later, in 1964, the town erected this delicious piece of historic kitsch to commemorate the occasion.

Railsplitter Covered Wagon
1750 Fifth St., Lincoln, IL

As the name suggests, the town of Lincoln has a bit of an obsession with the 16th president, as evidenced by the almost 25-foot-tall Railsplitter Covered Wagon—the world's largest covered wagon—where Abe himself can be found reading a law book. The wagon sits on the front lawn of a Best Western hotel.

ABOVE Railsplitter Covered Wagon

On the road . . .
Springfield

Illinois claims to be the home of the corn dog. To the brilliant soul who first dreamed of putting a corn dog on a stick, we salute you.

In 1837, the Springfield Road was constructed to connect St. Louis with Springfield, Illinois. The route became a popular stagecoach line for the next 20 years, but with the rise of the railroad, roads like this fell into disuse and disrepair. The advent of the automobile provided a welcome comeback, and by 1920 there were tens of thousands of cars on the road.

In 1925, the American Association of State Highway Officials approved a marking system for interstate

BELOW AND OPPOSITE Cozy Dog Drive In

routes. East–west routes were designated with even numbers and all ended with a 0, with one exception. After some controversy, mainly on the part of delegates from Kentucky, the route from Chicago to Los Angeles was given the number 66.

Cozy Dog Drive In
2935 S. Sixth St., Springfield, IL

While the corn dog technically wasn't invented here, the Cozy Dog Drive In claims to be where it was first put on a stick. Stop by to taste the original Cozy Dog, and don't forget to take a photo of it in front of the vintage sign.

Obed & Isaac's Microbrewery and Eatery
500 S. Sixth St., Springfield, IL

At Obed & Isaac's you'll find one of the more bizarre culinary confections that Illinois has to offer. The Horseshoe Sandwich is made with two slices of toast (usually Texas style), piled high with two burger patties, fries, and cheese sauce. A side order of seasoned fries is a must.

The Chili Parlor
820 S. Ninth St., Springfield, IL

If you're in the mood for a food challenge, head over to Joe Rogers' Chili Parlour and partake in the Firebrand Chili Challenge. See how many bowls of the famous extra-spicy chili you can eat. The current record is five.

The Pasfield House Inn

525 S. Pasfield St., Springfield, IL

For the full Lincoln experience, spend the night at the Pasfield House Inn in Springfield. This gorgeous, six-suite bed-and-breakfast is a Springfield landmark and oozes style. Owned and operated by Tony Leone, a local historian who greets his guests with that famous Prairie State hospitality, the inn sees quite a lot of visitors, especially history buffs on Lincoln-inspired pilgrimages. The Georgian-style home was built in 1896 and has been lovingly preserved under the care of Leone since 1996.

The inn's namesake, George Pasfield, was a banker who met Lincoln when they both lived in Springfield, and the two were involved in establishing the state capital in Springfield. As the patriarch of one of the wealthiest families in the city, Pasfield owned acres upon acres of land around the Illinois State Capitol.

The inn is within walking distance of the capitol and downtown Springfield. It is also close to the Cozy Dog (corn dogs and french fries are a totally acceptable breakfast). If you have time, reserve a spot on the spirited 90-minute, 10-block Lincoln Ghost Walk Tour. Springfield has a little something for everyone: History buffs, Route 66 aficionados, and foodies will all find something to love in the Land of Lincoln.

Our Lady of the Highways
22353 W. Frontage Road, Raymond, IL

The Shrine of Our Lady of the Highways has been watching over travelers since the 1950s. The I-55 / Route 66 shrine was originally made as a high school project. Stop at this beautiful roadside destination to pay homage to our guardian of asphalt, represented here by a statue bearing the inscription "Mary, Loving Mother of Jesus, Protect Us on the Highway."

Ariston Cafe
413 N. Old Route 66, Litchfield, IL

Thought to be one of the first restaurants on Route 66, Litchfield's Ariston Cafe is a roadside icon. Founded by Greek immigrant Pete Adam in 1924 (and moved to its current location in 1935), the cafe was placed on the National Register of Historic Places in 2006. The Adam family has been running the place for years, and the desserts are just as rich as the history.

Soulsby Service Station
710 W. First St., Mount Olive, IL

Located just 10 to 15 minutes down the road from Ariston Cafe, the Soulsby Station was designed and built in 1926 by Henry Soulsby. The building was designed to blend in with the surrounding residential area. Today, the station has been beautifully restored and is a popular stop for Route 66 travelers.

Henry's Rabbit Ranch
1107 Historic Old Route 66, Staunton, IL

Six miles south of Mount Olive, take a slight detour to Henry's Rabbit Ranch in Staunton. The ranch is full of Rabbits—both the Volkswagen kind (some stick out of the ground in a Stonehenge-like fashion) and the fluffy kind. If you're lucky, you might get to meet the owner and pet the real-life rabbits that spend their days hopping around the store. A short drive away is the St. Paul Lutheran Church with its large blue neon cross.

Pink Elephant Antique Mall
908 Veterans Memorial Drive, Livingston, IL

Pink Elephant Antiques is a treasure trove of quirky roadside attractions all in one place. Here you'll find vintage neon signage, fiberglass giants, and lots of other weird stuff. There's a cone-shaped ice-cream stand, a UFO-shaped 1960s Futuro

RIGHT Ice-cream stand at Pink Elephant Antique Mall

House, and, fittingly, a huge pink elephant. While there, stop at the on-site flea market, where you could easily spend several hours. For a bite to eat, hit up Weezy's Bar and Grill in nearby Hamel.

Luna Cafe
201 E. Chain of Rocks Road, Granite City, IL

Your last food-and-drink stop in Illinois should be Luna Cafe. Built in 1924, this Route 66 roadside joint was a favorite hangout and hideout for Al Capone. The neon sign alone is worth a visit, but the cold beer and good food make Luna the perfect place to stop before continuing into Missouri. The Luna Cafe is nothing fancy, but that's part of its appeal.

World's Largest Catsup Bottle
800 S. Morrison, Collinsville, IL

But wait—there are two more essential roadside stops before you leave Illinois: the World's Largest Catsup Bottle and the Cahokia Mounds. Originally built in 1949, the catsup bottle is an excellent example of roadside Americana, and thanks to a preservation group, it stands as tall and vibrant today as it did 70 years ago.

Cahokia Mounds State Historic Site
30 Ramey Drive, Collinsville, IL

Cahokia Mounds State Historic Site was once a heavily populated city that covered 6 square miles. Today, it clocks in at nearly 3.5 square miles, with 80 of the original 120 mounds remaining. This was the largest pre-Columbian settlement north of Mexico, and no other North American city surpassed it in size until the 1800s. Visitors can see the resting place of an important ruler (housed in Mound 72); a Cahokian version of Stonehenge (but with wooden poles instead of giant stones); and the public plaza, where

Cahokians played a highly competitive moving-target, spear-throwing game called Chunkey.

Pere Marquette State Park
13112 Visitor Center Lane, Grafton, IL

If you need one more outdoor adventure before heading into St. Louis, take a short hike around Pere Marquette State Park in Grafton. The park has 8,000 acres perfect for cycling, bird-watching, boating, picnicking, and camping.

BELOW Cahokia Mounds State Historic Site
RozenskiP/Shutterstock

On the road . . . Missouri

Many miles of Missouri's Route 66 have been replaced over the years by larger highways, so what remains of the original road is a patchwork, especially in and around St. Louis. The Show-Me State contains several abandoned stretches of the Mother Road, but it's still possible to travel on quite a bit of the original route. More than 300 miles of road takes you southwest from St. Louis to Joplin, a stretch packed with fantastic diners, classic roadside attractions, and classic photo ops.

Some say St. Louis deserves credit for inventing the ice-cream cone.

ABOVE Grand Falls in Joplin, Missouri

On the road . . .
St. Louis

Few cities are lucky enough to have an architectural icon like the Gateway Arch overlooking the mighty Mississippi River, but there's so much more to St. Louis. The city also has a booming craft brewery scene, a rich history, and top-notch cultural institutions.

Crown Candy Kitchen
1401 St. Louis Ave., St. Louis, MO

If you're in the mood for classic American grub, then stop by the historic Crown Candy Kitchen for some sweets and a classic counter lunch of sandwiches. The BLTs here are the stuff of legend, but the milkshakes are the real draw—you can't go wrong with a hot fudge or chocolate banana malted.

Gateway Arch National Park
11 N. Fourth St., St. Louis, MO

Gateway Arch National Park is so much more than just the iconic arch. There's also a free museum with exhibits detailing America's westward expansion and the building of the arch, which is a good place to start if you're waiting for your ride to the top (or if you're scared of heights but still want the arch experience). A trip to the top of the Eero Saarinen–designed monument—the world's tallest arch and the tallest man-made monument in the United States—offers great views of both sides of the Mississippi. Across the street is the Old Courthouse—site of the Dred Scott trial—which features an ornately decorated dome.

ABOVE The Gateway Arch
Oakley/Shutterstock

Weirdville

The Haunted Lemp Mansion
3322 DeMenil Place, St. Louis, MO

The Lemps were once one of the most influential families in St. Louis. Prohibition, divorce, death, and depression hit them hard, but most of the really dark stuff happened in their stately home, known as Lemp Mansion.

William Lemp had been grooming his son Frederick to take control of the family grocery business, but Frederick died at 28 from health complications. Shortly after, William's friend Frederick Pabst (yes, that Pabst) died. Less than two months later, William himself was found dead from a self-inflicted gunshot wound in the family mansion. Things only got worse from there: Two of William's remaining children also died by suicide and, because of Prohibition, the family's brewery closed.

William's son Charles continued to live in the house until the 1940s. He never married and was known for his strange behavior. He mailed a letter to a St. Louis funeral home with very specific instructions to be carried out upon his death: He wanted his remains transported to a crematory by ambulance and cremated immediately, and he requested that his body not be bathed, clothed, or altered in any way. He wanted his ashes to be placed in a wicker box and buried on his farm, without a funeral or death notice printed in the papers. Eight years later, he shot his dog and then himself, leaving behind a note saying, "St. Louis Mo/ May 9, 1949, In case I am found dead blame it on no one but me. Ch. A. Lemp."

Continued on next page

The ghosts of the Lemp family reportedly still haunt the mansion, now a dinner theater and bed-and-breakfast. Patrons frequently report seeing William's ghost peeking into bathroom stalls in the downstairs women's restroom and claim to have seen a spirit running up the stairs. Others hear horses outside or find that items have mysteriously moved across the room. A doorway in the basement leading to the beer storage caves is referred to as The Gates of Hell.

Brave travelers can book a stay in the mansion. If you're lucky, you might get to meet one of the Lemps and knock back a cold one—with a cold one.

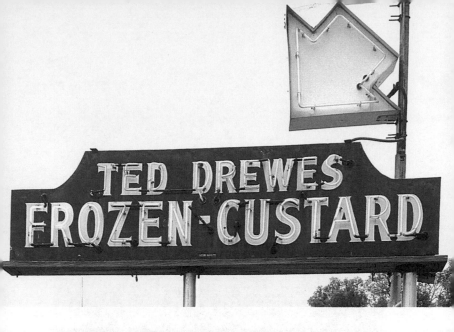

Ted Drewes Frozen Custard
6726 Chippewa St., St. Louis, MO

Ted Drewes Frozen Custard, a Route 66 icon, has been serving hot and hungry road travelers for more than 80 years. After opening his first successful custard store in Florida in 1929, Drewes opened a few more stores, including this stand located on Historic Route 66. Almost a century later, the stand is still a family-run business.

The Cheshire St. Louis
6300 Clayton Road, St. Louis, MO

The Cheshire is a British-themed hotel that may look out of place in St. Louis, but it's been a fixture in the city for close to a century. Dating back to the 1920s, the Cheshire is a charming throwback to traditional British inns, complete with a cozy on-site pub. A massive mounted bear, dark wood furniture, and wall tapestries greet you when you first walk in. A hot tip is to book the James Bond Suite.

ABOVE The Cheshire St. Louis hotel

Missouri was once home to the largest shoe manufacturer in the world, The Hamilton-Brown Shoe Factory.

48 hours in St. Louis

Whether you're staying at a galactic-themed hotel or getting lost in a phantasmagorical wonderland, St. Louis is an excellent weekend destination.

Gioia's Deli
1934 Macklind Ave., St. Louis, MO

St. Louis' Italian neighborhood is known as The Hill, and one of the most popular spots in the area is the James Beard award–winning Gioia's Deli. It has been open since 1918 (with a storefront purported to have been built with brick and wood from the 1904 World's Fair), and people still line up out the door for the incredible sandwiches. Most of the people in line will probably be ordering the hot salami (or the Salam de Testa, as it's sometimes called). The salami—hot in temperature, not spice—is made fresh daily and is absolutely worth the wait. Make sure to top it with ooey-gooey, melted Provel cheese (a St. Louis specialty made of cheddar, Swiss, and provolone) and *giardiniera* (Italian relish).

ABOVE Stained glass at St. Louis Union Station (see page 70)
Mobilus In Mobili/Flickr/CC BY-SA 2.0 (creativecommons.org/licenses/by-sa/2.0)

Dressel's Public House
419 N. Euclid Ave., St. Louis, MO

Wash down your Gioia's Deli hot salami with a beer or two at Dressel's Public House. With an impressive selection of craft beers, wine, and cocktails, this Welsh pub is a cozy place featuring rustic-chic decor and farm-to-table bar bites.

St. Louis Union Station
1820 Market St., St. Louis, MO

St. Louis Union Station looks like a castle, but it's actually a converted rail station. The building is stunning, inside and out—seriously, the lobby is drool-worthy. Inside is an aquarium, a variety of dining options (including a soda fountain that makes over-the-top shakes), a minigolf course, and much more. If you're not ready to leave, you can book a room at the St. Louis Union Station Hotel. Don't miss the hourly light show, projected onto the 65-foot ceilings each night from 5 to 10.

Moonrise Hotel
6177 Delmar Blvd., St. Louis, MO

Alternatively, you could check into the Moonrise Hotel, a funky boutique hotel with a galactic theme that promises to take guests on "a journey through space and time."

Rooster
1104 Locust St., St. Louis, MO

Nothing like a hearty brunch to start your day. Rooster offers a little something for every kind of brunch lover: traditional scrambles, sweet and savory crepes, French toast topped with caramelized bananas and nuts, and even a brunch burger.

Anheuser-Busch St. Louis Brewery
1 Busch Place, St. Louis, MO

Whether or not Budweiser is your beer of choice, there's no denying that its operation is impressive. Stop by the Anheuser-Busch brewery and take a tour. You can enjoy the General Brewery Tour, Beermaster Tour, or Day Fresh Tour, where you'll meet the Budweiser Clydesdales. Or just grab a brew in the beer garden.

Kim Lewis Photography/Shutterstock

ABOVE A Clydesdale horse at the Anheuser-Busch St. Louis Brewery

Pappy's Smokehouse
3106 Olive St., St. Louis, MO

St. Louis loves its barbecue, and Pappy's Smokehouse is one of the city's most beloved barbecue joints. It serves food only until it runs out—and the wait might be long—but once you taste the ribs or burnt ends, you'll understand why. There's also Frito pie, which includes cheddar cheese, baked beans, your choice of meat, and onions over a pile of Fritos. Trust us, it's delicious.

Soldiers Memorial Military Museum
1315 Chestnut St., St. Louis, MO

The St. Louis Soldiers Memorial Military
Museum was originally built to honor
local citizens who lost their lives in World
War I. This sobering and well-thought-out
museum includes uniforms, weapons, por-
traits, and art installations.

City Museum
750 N. 16th St., St. Louis, MO

City Museum describes itself as a "phantasmagorical
wonderland." Opened in 1997, the museum, housed
in an old shoe warehouse, contains found architectural and industrial objects, including a school bus,
cranes, a fire engine, and two old Saber F-86F aircraft
fuselages. There's also an aquarium, a Ferris wheel,
and a 10-story slide. But don't expect to have an easy
time finding any of it; the whole place is a maze of
exhibits, and there are no maps. Visitors are encouraged to explore and discover on their own. You never

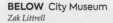

BELOW City Museum
Zak Littrell

know where a ladder or slide will take you—you could end up inside a life-size whale statue, at a giant skate park, in an enormous pit filled with balls, or in a tree house bar.

We toured the artsy and eccentric St. Louis playground and left more confused than when we arrived: **rt.guide/JFPU**

Schlafly Tap Room
2100 Locust St., St. Louis, MO

End your trip through St. Louis at one of the more famous craft breweries in town: the Schlafly Tap Room. In addition to pub food and delicious beers (try the grapefruit IPA or the oatmeal stout), the tap-room offers live music Thursday through Saturday.

BELOW Schlafly Tap Room
Flickr/Tom Bastin/CC BY 2.0 (creativecommons.org/licenses/by/2.0)

Grant's Farm
10501 Gravois Road, St. Louis, MO

Grant's Farm was built by General Ulysses S. Grant in the late 1840s. The property was later purchased by the Busch family (yes, the beer guys), and today it's a landmark open to visitors who want a beautiful spot to spend the afternoon. Guests can feed baby goats, take a tram ride through a wildlife preserve, and sample some beer. Admission is free, but there is a fee to park.

Laumeier Sculpture Park
12580 Rott Road, St. Louis, MO

On your way out of St. Louis, hit up the sprawling Laumeier Sculpture Park and museum. Stretch your legs among the weird and wild outdoor art exhibits, including a gigantic eyeball in the middle of a field.

St. Louis West/Historic Route 66 KOA
18475 Old US Highway 66, Eureka, MO

Looking for a place to camp for the night? The St. Louis West/Historic Route 66 KOA campground in nearby Eureka is located right on historic Route 66, just 30 minutes outside the city. (Also see page 37.)

You did it—one leg down, five more to go. As you travel farther southwest, the weather will get warmer, the road will get flatter, and the views will only get better.

While it's true that you never forget your first, so much of Route 66 is still in front of you—so keep going and let the Show-Me State show you why almost 100 years after its creation, the Mother Road is still the best place to get your kicks.

Leg 2:
St. Louis
to Tulsa

🅑 415 Miles

Find a complete Online Trip Guide
for leg 2:

rt.guide/ZTTF

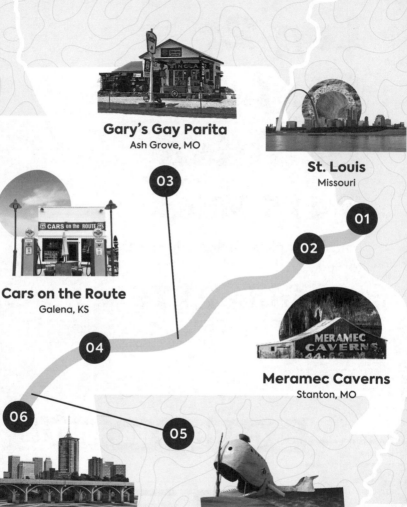

Gary's Gay Parita
Ash Grove, MO

St. Louis
Missouri

Cars on the Route
Galena, KS

Meramec Caverns
Stanton, MO

Tulsa
Oklahoma

Blue Whale of Catoosa
Catoosa, OK

01
02
03
04
05
06

Leg 2:
St. Louis to Tulsa

Route highlights

01 St. Louis

Meramec Caverns **02**

03 Gary's Gay Parita

Cars on the Route **04**

05 Blue Whale of Catoosa

Tulsa **06**

Featured campgrounds

Springfield/Route 66 KOA Holiday
5775 W. Farm Road 140, Springfield, MO

Relax at the end of the day by cooling off in the pool or playing a game of tetherball. RV sites, cabins, and tent sites are available. (Also see page 96.)

Route 66 RV Park
9755 OK 66, Sapulpa, OK

This is a small, clean, and quiet RV campground located on historic Route 66 and just minutes from downtown Tulsa. There are 34 sites and one apartment perfect for a quick overnight stay.

Featured accommodation

Best Western Route 66 Rail Haven
203 S. Glenstone Ave., Springfield, MO

This iconic Route 66 roadside motel puts you within reach of popular tourist attractions like Gary's Gay Parita and Pythian Castle.

On the road . . .
Missouri

Next up is St. Louis to Tulsa, a stretch that some travelers consider the heart of Route 66. It's where east meets west, linking up the Midwest with the West Coast. Much of this stretch is on I-44, which means lots of exits and county roads, but the scenery is often beautiful. When possible, we'll point out places where you can hop on and off the original parts of Route 66.

Playlist
Listen here: rt.guide/BBNU

Songs to get you in the mood while on the road . . .

1. "Fortunate Son," Creedence Clearwater Revival

2. "A Horse with No Name," America

3. "Highway to Hell," AC/DC

4. "Route 66," Chuck Berry

5. "Roadhouse Blues," The Doors

6. "Free Bird," Lynyrd Skynyrd

7. "On the Road Again," Canned Heat

8. "St. Louis Blues," W. C. Handy, Louis Armstrong

9. "The Heart of Rock and Roll," Huey Lewis & The News

10. "Country Grammar," Nelly

11. "A Mind with a Heart of Its Own," Tom Petty

12. "St. Louis Boogie," Count Basie Orchestra

13. "Okie From Muskogee," Merle Haggard

14. "Crazy About Oklahoma," Jimmy Reed

15. "24 Hours from Tulsa," The Bridgettes

ABOVE Artifacts attributed to Jesse James were found in Meramec Caverns, giving it the name Jesse James Hideout.

Meramec Caverns
1135 Highway W, Stanton, MO

If you're traveling during the summer months, this nice and cool detour will help you escape the heat. The 4.6-mile-long cave system is one of the Ozarks' coolest (literally and figuratively) natural wonders, as well as an archaeological hotbed of Native American artifacts.

Extra stops

Big Chief Roadhouse *Restaurant*
17352 Manchester Road, Glencoe, MO

Route 66 State Park *Attraction*
1628 97 N. Outer Road, Eureka, MO

Weirdville

Morse Mill (Haunted) Hotel
8850 Morse Mill Spur Road, Morse Mill, MO

Twenty miles southeast of St. Clair, you will find the Morse Mill Hotel, an alleged vortex of paranormal activity. This pre–Civil War hotel was constructed in 1816 as a simple farmhouse. Forty years later, a man named John Morse turned it into a four-story building made of maple, oak, cypress, and limestone. During the 1920s and '30s, the hotel was buzzing with activity as the place where the wealthy citizens of St. Louis escaped for a weekend getaway. Famous—and infamous—guests, including Charles Lindbergh and Al Capone, came from all over the world. Today, guests report hearing phantom footsteps and feeling apparitions brush up against them.

ABOVE An interactive walking museum of the notorious outlaw

Jesse James Wax Museum
I-44, Exit 230, Stanton, MO

The Jesse James Wax Museum in Stanton is an interactive walking museum that takes visitors through the life and mysterious death of the notorious outlaw. The gift shop is loaded with kitschy James memorabilia. The nearby Riverside Wildlife Center, full of snakes and alligators, is also worth a visit.

Extra stops

**Shaw Nature Reserve and
Joseph H. Bascom House** *Attractions*
307 Pinetum Loop Road, Gray Summit, MO

Lewis Cafe *Restaurant*
145 S. Main St., St. Clair, MO

Onondaga Cave State Park
7556 Highway H, Leasburg, MO

Onondaga Cave State Park is less famous—and less
crowded—than Meramec Caverns but is equally
impressive. Massive stalagmites and stalactites
drip from the ceiling and rise up from the floor, and
guided tours take visitors throughout the underground labyrinth. Don't miss the panoramic vista
points where you can get a great shot of the Meramec
River.

ABOVE The Lily Pad Room at Onondaga Cave State Park
Aneta Waberska/Shutterstock

Belmont Vineyards
5870 Old Route 66, Leasburg, MO

Enjoy a wine tasting at Belmont Vineyards, about
8 miles down the road from Onondaga Cave State
Park. This family-run business is a hidden gem in
the Ozarks, located between downtown Cuba and
Leasburg along historic Route 66 (an easy on-off
from I-44). Belmont frequently features live music on
weekends, and visitors can enjoy wine tastings and
good food with a beautiful view.

On the road . . .
Cuba

Nicknamed Route 66 Mural City, Cuba, Missouri, will
make you feel as if you've traveled back in time. The
town was founded in 1857 and named after the island
nation just south of Florida. Over the years, Cuba has
seen its fair share of famous visitors—including Bette
Davis, Amelia Earhart, and President Harry S. Truman—
many of whom are featured in the town's murals.

19 Drive-In
5853 MO 19, Cuba, MO

If you need a break from driving and sightseeing,
catch a flick at the 19 Drive-In. The classic theater
opened in 1955 and is still operating seasonally, from
March to October.

Wagon Wheel Motel
901 E. Washington St., Cuba, MO

In Cuba you'll find the iconic Wagon Wheel Motel, a
19-room Route 66 motel in operation since 1936.
Don't miss nearby vintage gas stations such as the
Old Conoco Service Station and a Phillips 66 station.

ABOVE From 1908 to 1954, this building served as the jail for Cuba.

Cuba City Jail
Prairie St. and the 300 block of
S. Main St., Cuba, MO

On the southwest corner of Prairie Street and South Main Street, you'll find a concrete block that served as the town's jail from 1908 to 1954. Today, the building is furnished with traditional prison furniture, including a wood cot and desk and a wood-burning stove.

Murals of Cuba, Missouri
Various locations, Cuba, MO

There are so many Route 66 icons to see and experience while in Cuba, but it's absolutely essential to take a tour of the famous Route 66 Viva Cuba murals. Take a journey through the town's history via 12 outdoor murals. For a more in-depth look, a narrated bus tour departs from the Cuba Visitor Center. A self-guided map is available at cubamomurals.com.

Lukasz Szwaj/Shutterstock

DETOUR

Missouri's mini wine country along Route 66

This part of Missouri is a small-scale wine country. Peaceful Bend, Rosati, and St. James wineries are within a 30-minute drive of one another, making the area a perfect place to stay for a few days.

Peaceful Bend Winery
1942 Highway T, Steelville, MO

Rosati Family Winery
22050 Highway KK, Rosati, MO

St. James Winery
540 Highway B, James, MO

Extra stops

Missouri Hickory Bar-B-Que _Restaurant_
913 E. Washington St., Cuba, MO

Shelly's Route 66 Cafe _Restaurant_
402 S. Lawrence St., Cuba, MO

Old Pulaski County Courthouse Museum
301 Route 66 E., Waynesville, MO

In Waynesville you'll find the Pulaski County Courthouse, a Romanesque Revival–style building built in 1903. Today, it serves as a museum and is a favorite photo op for history and architecture buffs.

ABOVE The world's second-largest rocking chair
Courtesy of Missouri Historical Society

The 40-foot-tall rocking chair in Fanning, Missouri, was once Guinness-certified as the world's largest rocker. In 2015, it was bumped down to second place by an even larger chair in Casey, Illinois.

DETOUR

Ha Ha Tonka State Park

1491 State Road D, Camdenton, MO

You may not expect to stumble upon the abandoned ruins of a castle in the middle of the Ozarks, but when driving down Route 66, this amazing state park is well worth the detour. Tucked behind lush forests and bordered by a vast lake, Ha Ha Tonka State Park is a world unto itself. The name Ha Ha Tonka reportedly comes from an Native American phrase for "laughing waters," a reference to the area's many springs. There are 17 miles of trails that feature sinkholes, natural bridges, caves, a spring, and the ruins of an early-20th-century castle.

Above: Jon Manjeot/Shutterstock

ABOVE Ruins at Ha Ha Tonka State Park

Robert McClure Snyder was born into a family of millers and grocers in 1852. Snyder moved to St. Louis to work in the grocery business, and in 1904 he bought 5,000 acres of land around Ha Ha Tonka Lake and Spring. He started building roads and exploring the caves, and he visited the area whenever he needed to escape his busy city life.

Snyder employed Scottish stonemasons to build his dream home, a massive, European-style castle with an incredible view overlooking the Lake of the Ozarks. But in 1906, before his dream home was completed, Snyder died in a car accident, becoming one of Missouri's

DETOUR

first automobile fatalities. In Snyder's obituary, the *Kansas City Journal* wrote that he "was a man who understood big things and made them win by keeping up the fight when other men might have been ready to give it up."

His sons took over construction of the castle and completed it in the 1920s. The castle was used as a residence for most of the next two decades until it became a boutique hotel in 1937. In 1942, a fire completely destroyed the interior and carriage house.

Ha Ha Tonka became an official state park in 1978, and visitors to the stabilized castle can still enjoy the artistic masonry of the ruins.

Route 66 Museum
915 S. Jefferson Ave., Lebanon, MO

The Route 66 Museum is a fun stop where visitors can view a reconstructed retro motel room, a gas station, and a diner. Admission is free, but donations are welcome.

Redmon's Candy Factory
330 W. Pine St., Phillipsburg, MO

If you need a sugar fix, stop in at Redmon's Candy Factory in Phillipsburg. They make more than 20 flavors of fudge and 70 flavors of taffy on site.

Extra stops

Starlite Lanes *Attraction*
1331 Route 66, Lebanon, MO

Munger Moss Motel *Accommodation*
1336 Route 66, Lebanon, MO

Wrink's Market *Photo Op*
135 Wrinkle Ave., Lebanon, MO

BELOW Get close to the animals on a driving tour at Wild Animal Safari.
Huw Penson/Shutterstock

ABOVE Hubble Telescope replica statue

Hubble Telescope Replica Statue
100 S. Clay St., Marshfield, MO

Edwin Powell Hubble was born in Marshfield in 1889. On the west side of the town square, a Hubble telescope replica statue commemorates the famous astronomer. It weighs a whopping 1,200 pounds and is a quarter of the size of the actual Hubble Space Telescope. The town itself is cute, too, so if you have time, spend a day strolling around.

Wild Animal Safari
124 Jungle Drive, Strafford, MO

The Wild Animal Safari in Strafford is a drive-through safari park with more than 65 types of exotic animals. You can also take a bus tour through the park or stretch your legs and visit the park's petting zoo, a fun way to break up the trip (and a big hit with kids).

On the road . . .
Springfield

Springfield is known both as the Queen City of the Ozarks and the Birthplace of Route 66. Located in south-central Missouri at a strategic crossroads, Springfield was a railroad hub, home to a bloody Civil War battle, and played an important role in the birth of the Mother Road. Route 66 was aligned through the city in 1926 and realigned in 1936. It funneled travelers to the many motels and businesses located along the way until I-44 bypassed the city in 1958.

Fantastic Caverns
4872 N. Farm Road 125, Springfield, MO

If you need a break from driving, pull over at Fantastic Caverns in Springfield and explore an underground world. North America's only completely ride-through cave tour is absolutely worth the 55-minute tram ride.

ABOVE Springfield's Central Square
Ted PAGEL/Shutterstock

ABOVE Pythian Castle

Pythian Castle
1451 E. Pythian St., Springfield, MO

Pythian Castle is frequently listed as one of the best-kept secrets in Missouri. Built in 1913 by the mysterious Knights of Pythias, the castle was ultimately purchased by the U.S. military and even housed some POWs during World War II. Today, it's privately owned and used for historic tours, ghost hunts, escape-room events, and murder mysteries.

Best Western Route 66 Rail Haven
203 S. Glenstone Ave., Springfield, MO

Don't miss the Best Western Route 66 Rail Haven hotel in Springfield. This classic roadside hotel has been a Mother Road fixture since 1938. There are several great photo ops around it, including an old-school fire truck and vintage gas pumps. One of the hotel's claims to fame is that Elvis Presley stayed here, and if it's good enough for The King, it's good enough for all of us.

Springfield/Route 66 KOA Holiday
5775 W. Farm Road 140, Springfield, MO

The Springfield/Route 66 KOA is located in the heart of the Ozarks, just 15 minutes from Fantastic Caverns and historic Wilson's Creek National Battlefield. You can get pizza delivered to your campsite, RV, or cabin.

Gary's Gay Parita
21118 Old 66, Ash Grove, MO

At this re-creation of a 1930 Sinclair gas station, you will find a wealth of information for the Route 66 roadie. Here, proprietor Gary Turner shares his knowledge of and love for the Mother Road with all who stop by, taking travelers on a journey in time. Along with the replica station, the site features original fuel pumps and other memorabilia from the heyday of Route 66.

Springfield, Missouri, is home to the flagship Bass Pro Shops Outdoor World location, which features a four-story waterfall. Next door is the award-winning Wonders of Wildlife National Museum and Aquarium.

Extra stops

1926 Gillioz Theatre *Attraction*
325 Park Central E., Springfield, MO

History Museum on the Square *Attraction*
154 Park Central Square, Springfield, MO

Birthplace of 66 Roadside Park *Attraction*
1200 W. College St., Springfield, MO

Wilder's Steakhouse *Restaurant*
1216 S. Main St., Joplin, MO

Granny Shaffer's *Restaurant*
2728 N. Rangeline Road, Joplin, MO

On the road . . .
Carthage

To drum up advertising for the Boots Court motel, located at 107 S. Garrison Ave. in Carthage, the owners broadcasted a message to listeners on the radio that encouraged road-weary travelers to have "breakfast at the Crossroads of America." This was a reference to the intersection of two major highways at Central and Garrison Avenues. Highways 66 and 71 presented the town with a major tourism boom, particularly in the post-Depression era, until the 1960s when I-44 was built just south of town. Recently the town has started to flourish once again. There are quite a few draws for tourists interested in both Route 66 sites and Victorian architecture.

Mother Road Coffee
325 S. Main St., Carthage, MO

If you're more into beans than brews, hit up Mother Road Coffee in Carthage. In addition to espresso and Italian sodas, you'll find a great selection of pastries and friendly baristas.

ABOVE Boots Court motel

Precious Moments Chapel
4321 S. Chapel Road, Carthage, MO

The Precious Moments Chapel in Carthage, often compared to Michelangelo's Sistine Chapel in Rome, is the love child of artist Samuel Butcher. Free tours are offered every day. The gift shop is considered to be the world's largest Precious Moments gift shop.

BELOW Precious Moments Chapel

Karen Montgomery/Flickr/CC BY-SA 2.0 (creativecommons.org/licenses/by-sa/2.0)

66 Drive-In Theatre
17231 Old 66 Blvd., Carthage, MO

By this point, you've likely passed a few drive-in theaters, and it's worth stopping at one to catch a movie. The 66 Drive-In in Carthage is a great surviving example of postwar outdoor theaters. Situated on a 9-acre, scenic plot of land, just about 3 miles from downtown, the drive-in (with a 66-foot-high screen, a playground, and an Art Deco concession stand) opened in 1949.

On the road . . .
Kansas

The Kansas section of Route 66 is short but sweet and manages to pack in several must-see stops in a little under 14 miles (13.2, to be exact). This small stretch passes through three towns—Galena, Riverton, and Baxter Springs—and can be driven in as little as 30 minutes. Kansas is the only state on your journey where the Mother Road isn't interrupted by the interstate. Don't miss the only remaining Marsh Arch Rainbow Bridge, several museums, and other small businesses; on Kansas' stretch of Route 66, you'll find quality over quantity.

BELOW AND OPPOSITE Grab a snack and peruse Route 66 memorabilia and old trucks at Cars on the Route.

On the road . . .
Galena

Galena is one of the best-preserved towns along Route 66. Home to the Kan-O-Tex gas station from Disney's *Cars*, the Murals of Galena, and a 1952 Will Rogers marker, Galena was once a successful mining town but was hit hard by the Depression and violent miner strikes. Later, when the town was bypassed by I-44, tourists stopped visiting, the mines closed down, and the population dropped. Today, several historical buildings around town offer a peek into Galena's rocky past.

Cars on the Route
119 N. Main St., Galena, KS

If you're coming in from Joplin heading west, your first stop in Galena should be Cars on the Route, a restored Kan-O-Tex service station formerly known as 4 Women on the Route. Along with snacks and sandwiches, it has antiques and Route 66 memorabilia made by local artists. Outside is a lineup of old trucks on display, including one that inspired the Tow Mater character in Disney's *Cars*.

ABOVE The Galena Mining Museum occupies an old railroad depot.
Tony Hisgett/Flickr/CC BY 2.0 (creativecommons.org/licenses/by/2.0)

Galena Mining and Historical Museum
319 W. Seventh St., Galena, KS

Hop over to the Galena Mining and Historical Museum to learn all about the region's rich mining history. The hours of the museum vary, but it's a fun stop full of newspapers from yesteryear and other antiques, including a collection of Model Ts and Model As in the back garage. The all-volunteer staff works tirelessly to preserve Galena's Route 66 history.

Old Riverton Store
7109 SE Oriole Lane, Riverton, KS

Heading out of Galena you'll hit the small town of Riverton, home to the Old Riverton Store. The building is a replica of the original building that was destroyed by a tornado in the 1920s. Here's another chance to buy both souvenirs and sandwiches.

ABOVE Rainbow Bridge over Brush Creek   *Ingo 70/Shutterstock*

Rainbow Bridge
Route 66, Baxter Springs, KS

Make sure to stop and take a photo at the Rainbow Bridge, also known as the Brush Creek Bridge. At one time, there were quite a few of these Marsh Rainbow Arch bridges along the route, but this beautiful 130-foot bridge, built in 1923, is now the only one still standing on the Kansas portion of Route 66.

You can take a picture standing in three states at the Tri-State Marker where Kansas, Oklahoma, and Missouri all meet at one point on a dead-end road a few miles off Route 66.

Extra stop

Galenas Murder Bordello *Museum*
206 N. Main St., Galena, KS

BELOW Galenas Murder Bordello, where up to 30 murders are said to have taken place in the late 1800s, is now a museum.

On the road . . . Oklahoma

Oklahoma takes pride in, and embraces, most of its nearly 400 miles of Route 66. There are more drivable portions of the old Mother Road in Oklahoma than in any other state, and plenty of reasons to stop the car along the way. The stretch from Quapaw to Texola is home to the Blue Whale of Catoosa, Art Deco gems of Tulsa, and two excellent museums filled with Route 66 history. Don't forget to stop at the Sandhills Curiosity Shop in Erick and say hi to Harley Russell—if you're lucky, he might serenade you with a round of "(Get Your Kicks on) Route 66," or hand you a guitar so you can play along.

Extra stops

Waylan's Ku-Ku Burger *Restaurant*
915 N. Main St., Miami, OK

Coleman Theatre *Attraction*
103 N. Main St., Miami, OK

Chelsea Motor Inn *Accommodation*
325 E. Layton St., Chelsea, OK

Pryor Creek Bridge *Attraction*
58 S4260 Road, Chelsea, OK

ABOVE Tulsa skyline *Sean Pavone/Shutterstock*

Weirdville

The Spook Light
Date: First reported in the 1800s
Location: 11 miles east of Quapaw, OK

The Spook Light is a creepy light or orb that has been sighted on County Road E-50 since at least the 1800s. Is it haunted headlights? Paranormal high beams? Or simply lost souls wandering Route 66 reminiscing about the good ol' days? Explanations range from the plausible to the bizarre.

Meet the 19-year-old budding entrepreneur who is helping restore his hometown's Route 66 legacy: **rt.guide/BBHN**

ABOVE Clanton's Cafe

Clanton's Cafe
319 E. Illinois Ave., Vinita, OK

Clanton's Cafe is an iconic Route 66 restaurant known for its breakfast and local cuisine. Menu highlights include the world-famous chicken-fried steak and calf fries (also known as Rocky Mountain oysters). It's home-cooked comfort food at its best.

Ed Galloway's Totem Pole Park
21300 OK 28A, Foyil, OK

Stop at the Totem Pole Park in Foyil to check out the world's largest concrete totem pole. This 14-acre park, consisting of 11 structures, was the brainchild of Ed Galloway, a retired art teacher. There are more than 200 bas-relief images on the totem pole, including Native American motifs, symbols, and animal figures. (See page 112 for a photo.)

Will Rogers Memorial Museum
1720 W. Will Rogers Blvd., Claremore, OK

At the Will Rogers Memorial Museum in Claremore, you'll find artifacts, memorabilia, and speeches from the actor, vaudeville performer, cowboy, humorist, newspaper columnist, and social commentator. You can even watch Rogers' movies in the on-site theater. This is a special spot for all the Will Rogers superfans out there (yes, they do exist).

RIGHT Statue at Will Rogers Memorial Museum
MWaits/Shutterstock

Weirdville

The Oklahoma Octopus

The Oklahoma Octopus is, allegedly, a massive, freshwater cephalopod with red skin and long tentacles that stalks unsuspecting swimmers at various lakes across the state. The cryptid has reportedly been sighted in freshwater, man-made lakes such as Lake Thunderbird, Lake Oologah, and Lake Tenkiller.

No known video or photographic proof of the octopus exists, but believers point to the strangely high mortality rates at the lakes as evidence of its existence (skeptics claim that these drownings are just the result of drunken accidents).

The Blue Whale of Catoosa

SPOTLIGHT

2680 N. US 66, Catoosa, OK

You've finally made it to one of the most popular attractions along Route 66. The Blue Whale of Catoosa was built by Hugh Davis in the early 1970s as a surprise anniversary gift for his wife, Zelta, who loved whales and collected whale figurines. Take time to wander around the remnants of this famed roadside wonder, and have a snack at one of the picnic tables.

Extra stops

Claremore Motor Inn *Accommodation*
1709 N. Lynn Riggs Blvd., Claremore, OK

J. M. Davis Arms and Historical Museum
*Attraction (home to the world's largest
private firearms collection)*
330 N. J. M. Davis Blvd., Claremore, OK

The Nut House *Shop*
26677 S. Route 66, Unit A, Claremore, OK

Molly's Landing *Restaurant*
3700 N. Old Highway 66, Catoosa, OK

Tulsa Port of Catoosa *Attraction*
5350 Cimarron Road, Catoosa, OK

D. W. Correll Museum *Attraction*
19934 E. Pine St., Catoosa, OK

BELOW Tulsa Port of Catoosa

Courtesy of Tulsa Port of Catoosa

ABOVE Ed Galloway's Totem Pole Park (page 108)

Ending this leg at the Blue Whale makes for a Route 66 highlight, but you still have plenty more attractions—and more than half of the Mother Road—ahead of you. Rest up, and get ready for more kitschy fun ahead.

Leg 3: Tulsa to Amarillo

📍 **372 Miles**

Find a complete Online Trip Guide for leg 3:

rt.guide/UJNM

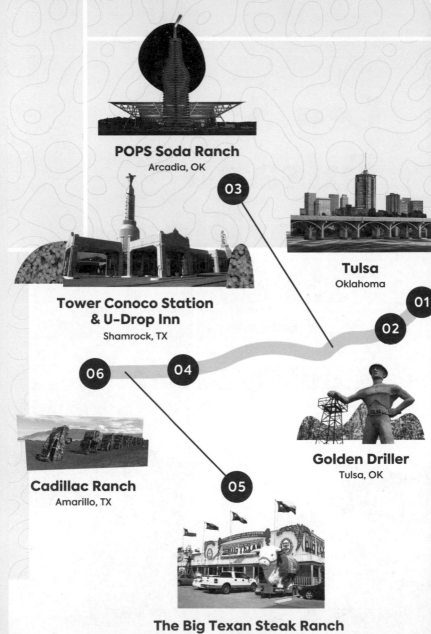

POPS Soda Ranch
Arcadia, OK

03

Tulsa
Oklahoma

01

02

Tower Conoco Station & U-Drop Inn
Shamrock, TX

06

04

Golden Driller
Tulsa, OK

Cadillac Ranch
Amarillo, TX

05

The Big Texan Steak Ranch
Amarillo, TX

Leg 3: Tulsa to Amarillo

Route highlights

01 Tulsa

Golden Driller **02**

03 POPS Soda Ranch

Tower Station and U-Drop Inn Café **04**

05 The Big Texan Steak Ranch

Cadillac Ranch **06**

Featured campgrounds

Twin Fountains RV Park
2727 NE 63rd St., Oklahoma City, OK

This RV resort has a bar and grill, a pool, a hot tub, and a splash pad. There's even a limo service if you need a lift to the OKC Zoo or Cowboy Hall of Fame.

Big Texan RV Ranch
1414 Sunrise Drive, Amarillo, TX

This campground has tent and RV sites and is located right next to the Big Texan Steak Ranch (see page 148). There's also a heated indoor pool.

Featured accommodation

Skirvin Hilton Hotel
1 Park Ave., Oklahoma City, OK

This is not your typical Route 66 roadside motel. If you like spooky ghost stories and sleepless nights, it's where you should stop for the night when passing through Oklahoma City.

Playlist
Listen here: rt.guide/RCLY

Songs to get you in the mood while on the road . . .

1. "I Am a Man of Constant Sorrow," The Soggy Bottom Boys

2. "All the Time in the World," John Fullbright

3. "Homesick, Lonesome, Hillbilly Okie," Hank Thompson

4. "Oklahoma, USA," The Kinks

5. "Is This the Way to Amarillo," Neil Sedaka

6. "Brownsville Girl," Bob Dylan

7. "Two-Lane Blacktop," Rob Zombie

8. "Flyover States," In the Pines

9. "Amarillo," Gorillaz

On the road . . .

In addition to Tulsa's massive Golden Driller statue and the Tumbleweed Grill and Country Store, this stretch is home to some absolutely amazing retro Route 66 motels (even if you aren't staying, pull over for the vintage signage). A few of the more famous ones include the Desert Hills Motel in Tulsa, the Skyliner Motel in Stroud, and the Lincoln Motel in Chandler.

On the road . . .
Tulsa

Welcome to the self-proclaimed Oil Capital of the World. But there's so much more to Oklahoma than just what's underground—the Sooner State was also home to Cyrus Avery, known as the Father of Route 66. Avery was appointed to the federal board tasked with the creation of the Interstate Highway System in the 1920s, and it was Avery who campaigned to have Route 66 pass through Tulsa.

Admiral Twin Drive-In
7355 E. Easton St., Tulsa, OK

The Admiral Twin Drive-In opened in 1951 and had a capacity of 1,500 cars. Today, two screens are still open seasonally for travelers wishing to spend an evening back in the '50s.

Desert Hills Motel
5220 E. 11th St., Tulsa, OK

The Desert Hills Motel (opposite) is a 50-unit retro lodge that's been recently renovated. The neon signage is vintage perfection, showcasing two large, glowing green cacti that have been welcoming road-weary travelers since 1953.

Elote Cafe & Catering
514 S. Boston Ave., Tulsa, OK

Hungry travelers may be tempted to take on Elote Cafe's puffy taco challenge, where you eat as many puffy tacos—flour tortillas filled with air, then deep fried and stuffed—as you can in 90 minutes. The current champion managed to gobble down 23. Challenge accepted.

Arnold's Old Fashioned Hamburgers
4253 Southwest Blvd., Tulsa, OK

Arnold's Old Fashioned Hamburgers has been a Tulsa tradition for more than 30 years. If you're a burger enthusiast, this stop is a must. Every day, nearly 500 burgers are sold, and not just to locals—people flock from all over for the griddle-cooked, quarter-pound burgers with all the trimmings. Don't miss the double-patty burger with onion rings and a milkshake.

The Golden Driller, a 76-foot-tall sculpture of an oil worker, was once displayed inside, at the International Petroleum Exhibition Building at the Tulsa Fairgrounds. Designed to house very large equipment, the building is said to have the world's largest unobstructed interior volume—meaning there are no interior supporting columns or beams.

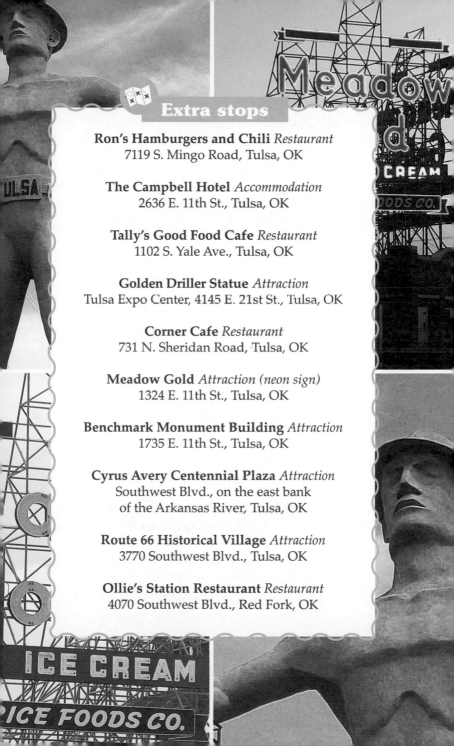

Ron's Hamburgers and Chili *Restaurant*
7119 S. Mingo Road, Tulsa, OK

The Campbell Hotel *Accommodation*
2636 E. 11th St., Tulsa, OK

Tally's Good Food Cafe *Restaurant*
1102 S. Yale Ave., Tulsa, OK

Golden Driller Statue *Attraction*
Tulsa Expo Center, 4145 E. 21st St., Tulsa, OK

Corner Cafe *Restaurant*
731 N. Sheridan Road, Tulsa, OK

Meadow Gold *Attraction (neon sign)*
1324 E. 11th St., Tulsa, OK

Benchmark Monument Building *Attraction*
1735 E. 11th St., Tulsa, OK

Cyrus Avery Centennial Plaza *Attraction*
Southwest Blvd., on the east bank
of the Arkansas River, Tulsa, OK

Route 66 Historical Village *Attraction*
3770 Southwest Blvd., Tulsa, OK

Ollie's Station Restaurant *Restaurant*
4070 Southwest Blvd., Red Fork, OK

John Frank House
1300 Luker Lane, Sapulpa, OK

The John Frank House—designed by Bruce Goff, a protégé of Frank Lloyd Wright's—is a beautiful crescent-shaped home with no sharp edges. Renowned potters John and Grace Lee Frank incorporated much of their signature style into the creation of their home, including hand-glazing all 2,500 tiles scattered throughout the house. The current caretakers, the Franks' daughters, frequently offer tours.

Extra stops

Giant Coke Bottle *Photo Op*
Frankoma Road and Route 66, Sapulpa, OK

Happy Burger *Restaurant*
215 N. Mission St., Sapulpa, OK

Tulsa-Sapulpa Union Railway Co. *Attraction*
701 E. Dewey Ave., Sapulpa, OK

Bristow Motor Co. *Photo Op*
500 N. Main, Bristow, OK

Bristow Museum *Attraction*
1 Railroad Place, Bristow, OK

VFW Post 3656 Wake Island Memorial *Attraction*
37033 Veterans Memorial Drive, Bristow, OK

Heart of Route 66 Auto Museum
13 Sahoma Lake Road, Sapulpa, OK

The Heart of Route 66 Auto Museum offers a short, fun respite from the road. The staff is eager to answer questions about the classic cars on display. Don't miss the museum's two vintage army jeeps (with mounted guns) and the 66-foot-tall gas pump outside.

BELOW Giant gas pump outside the Heart of Route 66 Auto Museum
Lina Holmes/Heart of Route 66 Auto Museum

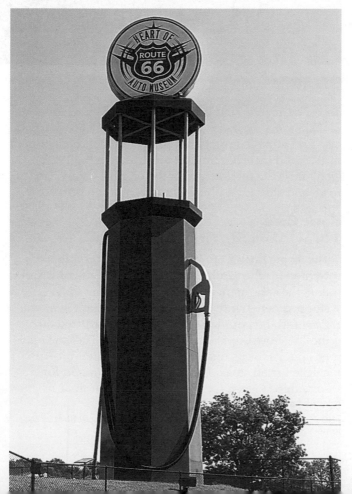

On the road . . .
Stroud

Take a moment to explore Stroud, a small town known as Oklahoma's winery and grape capital. Here you can also find unpaved segments of the original road, built in 1915 and incorporated into Route 66 in the 1920s. Don't miss the dirt section of the original Ozark Trail road, and stop for a photo and a BLT at the Rock Cafe.

Rock Cafe
114 W. Main St., Stroud, OK

The iconic Rock Cafe is a classic Route 66 stop. Named for the sandstone rocks used in its construction, the café opened in 1939. Crews from Pixar stopped here while they were researching the movie *Cars*, and the popular eatery was also featured on the TV show *Diners, Drive-Ins, and Dives*. The café may be famous for its mouthwateringly golden-brown chicken-fried steak, but if you're in the mood for something sweet, try the Diet Dr Pepper float.

ABOVE Order the chicken-fried steak or a Diet Dr Pepper float at the famous Rock Cafe.

Skyliner Motel
717 W. Main St., Stroud, OK

Also in Stroud, you'll find the retro-tastic Skyliner
Motel. This Route 66 staple features a vintage neon
sign pointing you in the right direction. The motel
is family-owned and within walking distance of the
Rock Cafe. After a long day of driving, check into
the Skyliner and walk to the restaurant—but keep in
mind they close at 6 p.m., so make it an early dinner.
Then hit up the nearby StableRidge Winery for a glass
of local vino.

BELOW Stay at the Skyliner and walk to the Rock Cafe for dinner.

On the road . . .
Chandler

As you drive through Chandler, take some time to see the town's murals and visit the Lincoln Motel, which has been in continuous operation since 1939. You'll also pass a historic Phillips 66 gas station and the Route 66 Interpretive Center, which is housed in a 1930s armory.

Lincoln Motel
740 E. First St., Chandler, OK

Chandler's Lincoln Motel was built in 1939 and has one of those motor courts you see in old movies. The cottage-style rooms are clean and comfortable. Even if you don't spend the night, it's worth pulling over to take a photo of the 1950s neon sign.

Route 66 Interpretive Center
400 E. US 66, Chandler, OK

At the Route 66 Interpretive Center, you'll be immersed in retro heaven. The center features frequently updated exhibits, films, and memorabilia,

BELOW Route 66 Interpretive Center
Wendy Kaveney/Jaynes Gallery/DanitaDelimont.com/Shutterstock

which sets it apart from other Route 66 museums. Here they've attempted to re-create the sights, sounds, and even smells of the Mother Road for a full sensory experience.

Phillips 66 Station #1423
701 S. Manvel Ave., Chandler, OK

Iconic Route 66 photo-op alert! There isn't anything to do at this filling station, but it's worth a stop to snap a picture of the classic type B cottage-style gas station built by Phillips Petroleum Company in 1930. The fun green color will look great in your Instagram feed.

Extra stops

McJerry's Route 66 Gallery *Attraction*
306 Manvel Ave., Chandler, OK

Lincoln County Museum of Pioneer History
Attraction
719 Manvel Ave., Chandler, OK

Boomarang Diner *Restaurant*
912 Manvel Ave., Chandler, OK

Seaba Station Motorcycle Museum *Attraction*
336992 E. OK 66, Warwick, OK

Captain Creek Bridge *Attraction*
Captain Creek Road, Wellston, OK

ABOVE The Old Round Barn is the route's only round wooden barn.
SBall/Shutterstock

The Old Round Barn
107 E. US 66, Arcadia, OK

The Old Round Barn was built in 1898, predating the construction of Route 66. In the late 1980s, the roof collapsed, but with the help of a group of mostly senior volunteers called the Over the Hill Gang, the barn was repaired and reopened as a landmark in 1992. It claims to be Route 66's only round wooden barn, and the ground level features historical displays and a gift shop.

POPS Soda Ranch
660 W. US 66, Arcadia, OK

After all that driving, you're probably thirsty. If carbonated refreshment is your jam, prepare to worship

ABOVE AND BELOW POPS Soda Ranch boasts more than 700 sodas.

at the altar of the POPS Soda Ranch. Located just off Route 66, it offers more than 700 sodas, sparkling waters, and shakes. Some of the more bizarre flavors include mustard, Buffalo wing, ranch dressing, and sweet corn. There's a 66-foot-tall soda bottle out front that lights up at night for a great photo op. This diner, gas station, and gift shop offers visitors several ways to "fill up."

On the road . . .
Oklahoma City

Oklahoma City (OKC) is the state's capital and the largest city you'll pass through on Route 66 in Oklahoma. It is home to many museums, memorials, and motels, in addition to a few stops worth a detour from the main route. Don't let the big-city vibe distract you from the fact that you're still in one of the most tornado-prone areas in the world. Since 1890, OKC has had about 150 tornados, so watch the skies and check the weather report if you're headed through in the spring or early summer.

National Cowboy & Western Heritage Museum
1700 NE 63rd St., Oklahoma City, OK

In Oklahoma City you'll find the National Cowboy and Western Heritage Museum, home to thousands of Western and Native American artworks and artifacts. Here you'll also find the world's largest collection of rodeo photographs, trophies, saddles, and barbed wire.

Arbuckle Mountain Fried Pies
3721 NW 50th St., Oklahoma City, OK

If you're ready for a life-changing culinary experience, hit up Arbuckle Mountain Fried Pies. These Oklahoma pies come from a tiny town called Springer, where Maude Pletcher perfected the family recipe and handed it down to her nine children. Decades later, Maude's grandson started selling the pies in their struggling gas station restaurant. The shop now offers fruit, chocolate, pumpkin, and coconut cream pies, along with sugar-free and savory pies.

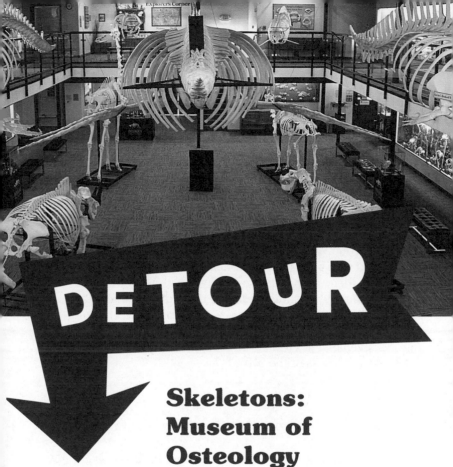

DETOUR

Skeletons: Museum of Osteology

10301 S. Sunnylane Road, Oklahoma City, OK
Although this isn't your standard Route 66 museum, Skeletons: Museum of Osteology, devoted to the study of bones, is still an interesting stop that features more than 350 animal skeletons from all over the world.

ABOVE Inside Skeletons: Museum of Osteology
Ayleen Dority/Flickr/CC BY 2.0 (creativecommons.org/licenses/by/2.0)

Skirvin Hilton Hotel
1 Park Ave., Oklahoma City, OK

If you're in the mood for a spooky evening, head to the Skirvin Hotel. Quaint hotels and motels near and on Route 66 have accommodated road travelers for decades, but stopping at a haunted hotel along the Mother Road may bring you face-to-face with some unexpected fellow guests. One of the creepiest haunted tales along the route is the story of Effie, the ghost of a maid said to have had an affair with oil tycoon W. B. Skirvin. Men staying at the hotel claim they've been propositioned by a female voice while in their rooms, and some say the ghost of a naked woman has showered with them during their stay. Others report creepy noises and maid carts moving down the halls on their own. The New York Knicks even blamed a 2010 loss to the OKC Thunder on the spookiness of the place.

Extra stops

Frontier City, a Six Flags Theme Park *Attraction*
11501 N. I-35 Service Road, Oklahoma City, OK

Oklahoma History Center *Attraction*
800 Nazih Zuhdi Drive, Oklahoma City, OK

Oklahoma City National Memorial and Museum *Attraction*
620 N. Harvey Ave., Oklahoma City, OK

Jack's Bar-B-Q *Restaurant*
4418 NW 39th St., Oklahoma City, OK

DETOUR

Tiger Safari Zoological Park

963 County Street 2930, Tuttle, OK

The Tiger Safari Zoological Park features more than 170 animals, a re-created African safari village, and the opportunity to spend the night in a safari hut. The three bush huts are set near a lagoon and come equipped with a queen-size bed, an air conditioner, and a large TV. There are also new tree houses available for lodging.

ABOVE Tree house lodging overlooking the animal habitats at Tiger Safari Park *William Meadows*

Sid's Diner
300 S. Choctaw Ave., El Reno, OK

Sid's Diner in El Reno is renowned for its fried-onion burger. What makes this burger so epic is both its size and its onions, which are caramelized directly onto the patty. You may recognize this dish from the Travel Channel show *Man v. Food*.

afumi1985/Flickr/CC BY-SA 2.0 (creativecommons.org/licenses/by-sa/2.0)

ABOVE Sid's Diner is famous for its burgers.

Red Rock Canyon Adventure Park
116 Red Rock Canyon Road, Hinton, OK

Just 1 mile south of Hinton, you'll find Red Rock Canyon Adventure Park. Native Americans used to set up camp here in the winter, and it was also once a major stop for 19th-century settlers who were heading west to California.

Lucille's Service Station
Old Route 66, Hydro, OK

Also known as Provine Station, this classic Route 66 gas station, built by Carl Ditmore in 1929, is one of only a few upper-story, porch-style stations left in the United States. Ditmore sold the station to the Hamons family, and Lucille Hamons ran it for 60 years, giving it its current name.

russellstreet/Flickr/CC BY-SA 2.0 (creativecommons.org/licenses/by-sa/2.0

ABOVE Lucille's Service Station is one of only a few of its kind in the U.S.

Stafford Air & Space Museum
3000 E. Logan Road, Weatherford, OK

Among the museum's more than 3,500 artifacts from the history of air and space travel are space suits worn by astronauts in orbit, nuclear missiles, a Titan II rocket, the *Gemini 6* space capsule, and a re-creation of the Wright Brothers' glider.

Jigg's Smokehouse
22203 N. Frontage Road, Clinton, OK

If you've had your fill of chicken-fried steak and are in the mood for some good barbecue, head to Jigg's Smokehouse, one of the most famous barbecue joints on the entire Mother Road. Established by Jiggs Botchlett, the smokehouse has been serving its signature secret recipe from a little hole-in-the-wall shack since the late 1970s.

Old Town Museum
2717 W. Third St., Elk City, OK

Learn more about early pioneer life at Elk City's Old Town Museum, located in a beautiful two-story Victorian home. The displays here focus on Americana and local history, including memorabilia from Susan Powell, 1981's Miss America and the pride of Elk City.

National Route 66 Museum
2717 W. Third St., Elk City, OK

Also in Elk City is the National Route 66 Museum. What makes this museum unique is its focus on the people who once lived and worked along Route 66. You can walk through each of the states along the route and through various eras while listening to recorded histories and personal accounts.

OPPOSITE Learn about the history of the route through personal accounts at the National Route 66 Museum.

Extra stops

Heartland Museum *Attraction*
1600 S. Frontage Road, Weatherford, OK

Best Western Plus Weatherford *Hotel*
525 E. Main St., Weatherford, OK

Cherokee Trading Post & Boot Outlet *Attraction*
23107 N. Frontage Road, Clinton, OK

White Dog Hill Restaurant *Restaurant*
22901 Route 66, Clinton, OK

Redland Theatre *Photo Op*
608 Frisco Ave., Clinton, OK

McLain Rogers Park *Attraction*
S. 10th St. and Bess Rogers Drive, Clinton, OK

Route 66 Mini-Golf *Attraction*
Jaycee Lane and S. 10th St., Clinton, OK

Oklahoma Route 66 Museum *Attraction*
2229 W. Gary Blvd., Clinton, OK

Tumbleweed Grill and Country Store
16726 Route 66, Texola, OK

The Tumbleweed Grill and Country Store in Texola is the last stop along Route 66 in Oklahoma. This general store and restaurant features home-cooked meals and calls itself Route 66's oldest working café. Formerly a 1930s dive bar, today the Tumbleweed is open daily for breakfast, lunch, and dinner, serving breakfast all day. Explore the border town of Texola—now a veritable ghost town—and don't miss the old Territorial Jail located on Main Street.

 Extra stops

Flamingo Inn *Accommodation*
2000 W. Third St., Elk City, OK

Western Motel *Accommodation*
315 NE US 66, Sayre, OK

66 Bar *Restaurant*
1601–1639 N. Third St., Sayre, OK

Sandhills Curiosity Shop *Attraction*
201 S. Sheb Wooley St., Erick, OK

100th Meridian Museum *Attraction*
101 S. Sheb Wooley St., Erick, OK

 Harley Russell, Route 66's most famous hillbilly hoarder, presides over Sandhills Curiosity Shop—a place where nothing is for sale: **rt.guide/ZVWV**

On the road . . . Texas

The Lone Star State has about 180 miles of old Route 66 road still remaining. It closely parallels I-40, so it's easy to hop on and off stretches of the Mother Road. The billboards along I-40 may not tell you this, but we will: Some of the very best roadside attractions in the U.S. are right here in the panhandle of Texas.

Extra stops

Western Motel *Accommodation*
104 E. 12th St., Shamrock, TX

Magnolia Gas Station *Attraction*
100–198 N. Texas St., Shamrock, TX

Blarney Stone *Attraction*
101–199 E. Second St., Shamrock, TX

Pioneer West Museum *Attraction*
204 N. Madden St., Shamrock, TX

ABOVE The midpoint of the route in Adrian, Texas
Ingo70/Shutterstock

Tower Station and U-Drop Inn Café

101 E. 12th St., Shamrock, TX

Miami's South Beach is lauded for its incredible Art Deco buildings, but did you know that one of the most beautiful examples of the style sits along a forgotten stretch of Route 66 in the little town of Shamrock, Texas? A once-bustling Conoco station and café, the Tower Station and U-Drop Inn Café still lights up the night with its stunning neon.

You may recognize Tower Station from the movie *Cars.* One of many locations in the movie based on real-life Route 66 icons, Ramone's House of Body Art (an auto body shop) is heavily inspired by the U-Drop Inn. Built in 1936, the inn was inspired by a drawing John Nunn made in the dirt with a nail. The gas station and café would become an enduring example of fine Route 66 architecture for roughly 60 years before closing.

The First National Bank of Shamrock purchased the building in 1999 and donated it to the City of Shamrock, which restored it with help from a $1.7 million federal grant. Today you can drop in to the gift shop and small museum.

Shamrock, Texas, used to be littered with the remains of the old Route 66 glory days, including an auto graveyard, a drive-in theater, and a campground.

Devil's Rope Museum
100 Kingsley St., McLean, TX

Devil's Rope is another name for barbed wire, which was invented in the late 1860s and was instrumental in settling the West. The Devil's Rope Museum in McLean is dedicated to the preservation of all types of barbed wire and includes historical documents, photos, and other memorabilia. Visitors are invited to "get hooked" on barbed wire, and while we hope that won't happen, it's still a fun stop.

BELOW More than 2,000 types of barbed wire have been found by collectors. Learn more fun facts about the Devil's Rope at this museum.

Extra stops

McLean-Alanreed Historical Museum *Attraction*
116 Main St., McLean, TX

Phillips 66 Gas Station *Attraction*
218 First St., McLean, TX

Cactus Inn Motel *Accommodation*
101 Pine St., McLean, TX

Red River Steakhouse *Restaurant*
101 Route 66, McLean, TX

Groom Cross
2880 County Road 2, Groom, TX

You're traveling through "God country," and the Groom Cross—a 190-foot-tall cross on the side of I-40—makes that very clear. At the foot of the cross, you'll see 14 life-size statues that represent the stations of the cross. The Groom Cross was featured prominently in the Steve Martin comedy *Leap of Faith*. Groom is also home to the Leaning Tower of Texas, originally a fully functional water tower that was later purchased by Ralph Britten to use as a marketing ploy for his truck stop. While in Groom, you can rest your weary head at the Chalet Inn, or grab a bite at The Grill.

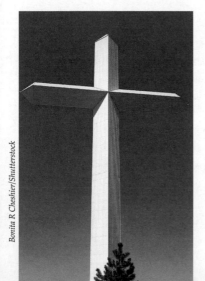

Bonita R Cheshier/Shutterstock

SPOTLIGHT

McLean, Texas

Located in Gray County, Texas, McLean is a virtual ghost town. As of 2000, according to the United States Census Bureau, the town had just under 830 residents. When planning your road trip, it's easy to miss McLean, a town that covers just 1.2 square miles. There aren't any iconic diners or motels still in operation, but the Red River Steakhouse claims to be the best-kept secret in Texas. The tiny town may fly under the radar, but we think it's one of the best-preserved, most enchanting ghost towns along Route 66.

ABOVE AND OPPOSITE Phillips 66 gas station in McLean

In 1901, Alfred Rowe, a rancher from England, donated his land to the town. Twelve years later, Rowe died aboard the RMS *Titanic*. Named after Judge William P. McLean, who served in the Texas legislature and on the Railroad Commission, McLean once had three general stores, livery stables, a lumberyard, a bank, wagon yards, and a local newspaper (*The McLean News*).

When Route 66 was built through the town in 1927, McLean became a popular stopover for tourists. Today, the McLean-Alanreed Historical Museum features exhibits on the town's once-booming livestock, agriculture, and oil industries. The population increased to about 1,500 by the 1940s, and the town boasted six churches, dozens of businesses, and a POW camp. In operation from 1942 to 1945, the camp housed thousands of German prisoners.

As nearby bigger cities such as Amarillo became more popular, business in McLean dwindled, the population decreased, and the construction of I-40 dealt the town its final blow. It is still home to a Phillips 66 on-the-route gas station, two museums, and the girls basketball team the McLean Tigers. The team recently placed second in the state tournament in Austin. Go Tigers!

VW Slug Bug Ranch
I-40 Frontage Road, Panhandle, TX

Just 30 minutes from Cadillac Ranch is the lesser-known, but just as interesting, VW Slug Bug Ranch. Here you'll find several vintage Volkswagen Beetles stuck into the ground alongside the remnants of an abandoned gas station. There are no signs advertising the ranch, but if you get off I-40 at Exit 96, you'll find it near three abandoned buildings. Plan on spending 15 to 20 minutes exploring and taking pictures. And don't forget your spray paint.

BELOW Add your own graffiti to the cars at the VW Slug Bug Ranch.

DETOUR

Palo Duro Canyon State Park

11450 Park Road 5, Canyon, TX

Get your nature kicks on Route 66 at Palo Duro Canyon State Park. This is the second-largest canyon in the U.S., and admission is only $8. You can easily drive the length of the park and pull over for the scenic overlooks. There's a sizable campground in the park (perfect for stargazing), and several trails that traverse the bottom of the canyon offer a beautiful place to stretch your legs.

ABOVE Take a hike or camp overnight at Palo Duro Canyon State Park.
Zack Frank/Shutterstock

Panhandle-Plains Historical Museum
2503 Fourth Ave., Canyon, TX

At the Panhandle-Plains Historical Museum, you can explore more than 14,000 years of Lone Star State history. The museum features dinosaurs, cowboys, pioneers, conquistadors, oil barons, and a life-size Old West Pioneer Town. This is a great place to spend an afternoon or a full day.

On the road . . .
Amarillo

When you reach Amarillo, you're nearly halfway through Route 66. Here you'll find cowboys and one of the largest livestock markets in the U.S. The Dust Bowl badly affected farmers here, and the Great Depression ended the prosperity brought by the oil boom, so when Route 66 was decommissioned, much of the Texas Panhandle was hit hard. On this stretch of the route, Amarillo is really the only major Panhandle town; otherwise you'll find plenty of virtual ghost towns.

Immigrant communities and Somalian cowboys are challenging stereotypes along the Mother Road: **rt.guide/CUMB**

The Big Texan Steak Ranch
7701 E. I-40 Access Road, Amarillo, TX

Everything is bigger in Texas, so you might as well try your luck with the 72-ounce steak challenge at

ABOVE Come hungry to The Big Texan Steak Ranch.

The Big Texan Steak Ranch in Amarillo. Just a few years after owner Bob Lee opened his steakhouse, he noticed an influx of hungry cowboys on payday looking to chow down on some hearty steaks. One Friday in 1962, Lee set up an eating contest to see who could eat the most 1-pound steaks in an hour. After one cowboy ate 72 ounces (along with a salad, a shrimp cocktail, a roll, and a baked potato), Lee declared that anyone who could eat that much steak in an hour should get it for free. The current record holder is Molly Schuyler, who devoured three steaks (plus sides) in just 20 minutes in 2015. The restaurant also features a shooting gallery, arcade games, a huge gift shop, and a bull statue out front.

Wonderland Amusement Park
2601 Dumas Drive, Amarillo, TX

The vintage Wonderland Amusement Park is a beloved family theme park that's been open since

1951. Frequently listed as one of the best amusement parks in Texas, the park includes more than 30 rides; miniature golf; and the Texas Tornado, a double-loop steel roller coaster. It's open on weekends from April to Labor Day, and weeknights from April to August.

BELOW With more than 30 rides, Wonderland Amusement Park has been beloved by Texans since 1951.

Courtesy of Wonderland Amusement Park | Amarillo, Texas

GoldenLight Cafe and Cantina
2906 SW Sixth Ave., Amarillo, TX

When you're ready for a cold beer and some good tunes, visit the GoldenLight Cafe and Cantina in Amarillo. It's a fantastic little roadhouse that serves up burgers and beers, often with a side of live music. The restaurant, which opened in 1946, has changed hands over the years, and its chili recipe has also changed with each subsequent owner. As the oldest restaurant in Amarillo, GoldenLight has developed quite the fanatic following over the years.

BELOW Catch some live music and have a bowl of chili at GoldenLight Cafe and Cantina

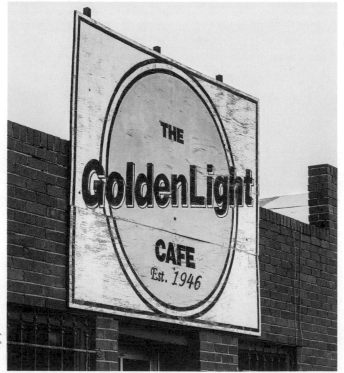

Courtesy of Amarillo CVC

Second Amendment Cowboy
2601 Hope Road, Amarillo, TX

The Second Amendment Cowboy proudly stands guard over Americans' right to bear arms—but you may notice that Mr. Second Amendment is strangely missing something: a gun. The cowboy was abandoned for years—and frequently used for target practice—until it was moved to Amarillo and restored. Standing more than 22 feet tall, the cowboy wears a large Stetson hat and is waving with his right hand, his left resting at his side. There's a fake historical marker in front of the statue that quotes the U.S. Constitution's Second Amendment.

BELOW Second Amendment Cowboy

Mark Collins/Flickr/CC BY 2.0 (creativecommons.org/licenses/by/2.0)

Cadillac Ranch and its changing colors

SPOTLIGHT

Ten Cadillacs stand along I-40, half-buried nose-down in the dirt at the same angles as the Pyramids of Giza. Visitors are encouraged to bring a can of spray paint and add their own mark to this unique roadside art installation.

Of all the roadside attractions in the U.S, Cadillac Ranch may be one of the most iconic and most photographed. Located just outside of Amarillo, the colorful Cadillacs have inspired travelers, filmmakers, and musicians. Today, spray-painting the cars is a rite of passage for any true roadtripper, and the installation has gone through quite a few makeovers throughout the years.

Erected in 1974 by three artists who called themselves the Ant Farm, and financed by eccentric millionaire Stanley Marsh 3 (he thought Roman numerals were too pretentious), Cadillac Ranch went relatively unnoticed for some time. Over the years, the Caddies became

Above: Bryan Brumley

a must-see roadside attraction, and the Ant Farm collective and Marsh 3 realized they could have a lot of fun (and support charities) by painting and repainting the cars. They've been painted pink on two occasions—once in 2005 to promote breast cancer awareness and once to celebrate the birthday of Marsh 3's wife, Wendy.

In 2002, the Ant Farm painted the cars back to their original colors, a project in conjunction with a larger Route 66 restoration project sponsored by Hampton Inn. The cars were painted white for a TV commercial, and tourists were thrilled to have 10 blank canvases to spray-paint when the commercial shoot was finished. In 2003, the cars were painted black to honor the passing of the Ant Farm's Doug Michels. But most of the time, you'll see the cars covered in various states of graffiti, and that's just the way the Ant Farm intended.

BELOW Aerial view of Cadillac Ranch
Courtesy of Amaraillo CVC

Weirdville

Why Amarillo is covered in cryptic road signs

You may notice some strange street signs on Amarillo's back roads. These are part of an art installation called the Dynamite Museum, funded in part by oil heir and patron of offbeat art Stanley Marsh 3 (of Cadillac Ranch fame). There were once dozens of signs, but people in town started to have mixed feelings about them around 2013, when Marsh 3 was indicted for allegedly assaulting two teenage boys; some of the signs were even taken down or painted over. Marsh 3 died in 2014, and new signs have not been installed for a while, but there are still plenty to discover, if you know where to look.

 The collection of painted traffic signs scattered across Amarillo, Texas, has nothing to do with actual rules of the road: **rt.guide/TCPT**

Tyler's Barbeque
3301 Olsen Blvd., Amarillo, TX

If you've got a hankering for barbecue, Tyler's is dry-rub heaven. Here, the ribs are smoked daily, and the brisket and pulled pork are truly mouthwatering.

Extra stops

U.S. Route 66–Sixth Street Historic District
Attraction Sixth Ave. between Georgia
and Forrest Aves., Amarillo, TX

The NAT (formerly known as the Natatorium)
Shop 2705 SW Sixth Ave., Amarillo, TX

Texas Ivy Antiques *Shop*
3511 SW Sixth Ave., Amarillo, TX

Courtesy of Amarillo CVC

ABOVE U.S. Route 66–Sixth Street Historic District

After Amarillo, you still have a little less than half of the Texas Panhandle to go before hitting New Mexico. The skies only get wider and the land drier as you head farther west. The "everything is bigger in Texas" attractions are mostly behind you, but there is plenty of small-town charm ahead.

Leg 4: Amarillo to Albuquerque

 291 Miles

Find a complete Online Trip Guide
for leg 4:

rt.guide/CMCT

Tee Pee Curios
Tucumcari, NM

03

BLUE HOLE
DEPTH 81 FT.
DIAMETER 60 FT.
OUTFLOW 3000
WATER-TEMP 61

Blue Hole of Santa Rosa
Santa Rosa, NM

Amarillo
Texas

06

05

01

02

Albuquerque
New Mexico

04

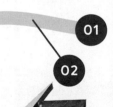

Blue Swallow Motel
Tucumcari, NM

MidPoint Cafe
Adrian, TX

Leg 4:
Amarillo to Albuquerque

Route highlights

01 Amarillo

MidPoint Cafe **02**

03 Tee Pee Curios

Blue Swallow Motel **04**

05 Blue Hole of Santa Rosa

Albuquerque **06**

Featured campgrounds

Santa Rosa Lake State Park Campground
NM 91, Santa Rosa, NM

This beautiful state park campground has a variety of reservable, walk-in, and primitive sites. It is open year-round, and reservations can be made up to six months in advance at reserveamerica.com.

Enchanted Trails RV Park & Trading Post
14305 Central Ave. NW, Albuquerque, NM

Located directly on historic Route 66, the Enchanted Trails RV Park & Trading Post is only minutes from Petroglyph National Monument and Volcanoes Day Use Area. There is also a charming collection of vintage RVs on-site, providing additional Route 66 vibes and photo ops.

ABOVE Blue Swallow Motel

Featured accommodation

Blue Swallow Motel
815 E. Route 66, Tucumcari, NM

Book a room with an attached garage, snap a photo of the neon sign, and sit on lawn chairs while the sun sets over the New Mexico desert. The Blue Swallow is a classic Route 66 experience. (Also see page 171.)

Playlist
Listen here: rt.guide/ADRV

Songs to get you in the mood while on the road . . .

1. "Texas," The Charlie Daniels Band
2. "Girls from Texas," Pat Green, Lyle Lovett
3. "Waltz Across Texas," Ernest Tubb
4. "Amarillo by Morning," George Strait
5. "Worse Comes to Worst," Billy Joel
6. "New Mexico Rain," South by Southwest
7. "Point Me in the Direction of Albuquerque," The Partridge Family
8. "O, Fair New Mexico," Rick Pickren
9. "Feels Like Home," Paul Richmond
10. "Radio America," The Libertines

On the road . . .

The stretch of I-40 between Amarillo, Texas, and Albuquerque, New Mexico, is fairly desolate. Aside from roadside truck stops and the occasional fast food chain, there's not much to see or do along this 280-mile open road, but just a few miles off I-40 is an opportunity to cruise through one of Route 66's most iconic towns: Tucumcari, New Mexico (see page 169).

ABOVE Neon sign and old chuck wagon in Tucumcari, New Mexico
Cheryl Gescheidle/Shutterstock

On the road . . .
Vega

The town of Vega sits right on historic Route 66 and has several landmarks worth stopping for. Also worth checking out are Dot's Mini Museum, Rooster's Mexican Restaurant & Cantina, Hickory Inn Cafe, Bonanza Motel, Vega Motel (built in 1947), and a restored Magnolia service station. As one of the sunniest places in the U.S., Vega is sometimes referred to as the Solar Capital of Texas.

Magnolia Station
222 N. Main St. (Coke St.), Vega, TX

The abandoned, vintage gas station makes for a great photo op, particularly as the sun is setting.

BELOW This Magnolia gas station was built in 1924, before Route 66 was established. *Barbara Brannon/Flickr/CC BY 2.0 (creativecommons.org/licenses/by/2.0)*

ABOVE Roosters Mexican Restaurant & Cantina

Roosters Mexican Restaurant & Cantina
1300 Vega Blvd., Vega, TX

Vega is home to Roosters, a small-town Mexican cantina easily accessed from I-40. Try the steak enchilada and fried ice cream.

Hickory Inn Cafe
1004 Vega Blvd., Vega, TX

Hickory Inn Cafe is an adorable spot in Vega, perfect for photos. Out front is a truck that looks like Mater from *Cars,* complete with a cow in the back. Stop in, grab an iced tea, and learn about the history of Vega.

Extra stops

Dot's Mini Museum *Attraction*
105 N. 12th St., Vega, TX

Oldham County Farm and Ranch
Heritage Museum *Attraction*
1100 Main St., Vega, Texas

MidPoint Cafe
305 W. Historic Route 66, Adrian, TX

Once you reach Adrian, pat yourself on the back: you've made it to the midpoint of Route 66. You'll know you've arrived once you see the MidPoint Cafe, a vintage-style roadside diner and gift shop with lots of photo ops to commemorate your journey down (half of) the Mother Road. The café claims to be located at the geographic midpoint between LA and Chicago.

ABOVE MidPoint Cafe

On the road . . .
New Mexico

New Mexico is known as the Land of Enchantment, and for good reason. There is certainly something enchanting about the Southwest. Maybe it's the combination of hot springs, forests, desert, and mountains, or the area's rich history and strong, visceral ties to the past. Towns such as Santa Fe and Taos are full of art galleries, boutiques, innovative architecture, museums, great restaurants, and more. There are some gorgeous side trips you can enjoy, including the High Road to Taos or a drive down the Turquoise Trail, a scenic byway that connects Santa Fe to Albuquerque. The trail commemorates the state's mining history as it passes through the stone-and-ore-laden mountains and former boom towns.

 A community of "voluntary anarchists" in Taos is taking off-the-grid living to the next level: **rt.guide/ATKG**

Glenrio, Texas–New Mexico state line
TX Loop 504/NM 1578

Once a bustling desert oasis built on the state line between Texas and New Mexico, today Glenrio is a ghost town. But just because the town is abandoned doesn't mean it's irrelevant. The Glenrio Historic District is listed on the National Register of Historic Places. It also has a place in pop culture: a scene for the film adaptation of *The Grapes of Wrath* was filmed here, and in the animated movie *Cars*, an abandoned "Glenn Rio Motel" is turned into a racing museum.

ABOVE Abandoned post office in Glenrio   *e-jewell wing/Shutterstock*

Russell's Travel Center
1583 Frontage Road 4132, Glenrio, NM

The next-level Russell's Travel Center is located right on Historic Route 66 and has everything a road traveler could possibly want, including an on-site grocery store, a retro diner, a classic-car museum, showers, and even a chapel.

Ute Lake State Park
1800 540 Loop, Logan, NM

If you need a break from driving, Ute Lake State Park in Logan features many miles of shoreline (the lake itself is 13 miles long), RV sites, and a campground where you can sleep under the stars. It's a peaceful spot to recharge before getting your kicks in Tucumcari.

ABOVE Ute Lake State Park   *Jon Manjeot/Shutterstock*

On the road . . .
Tucumcari

Tucumcari is an iconic Route 66 town full of retro signage, abandoned motels, and classic diners that's actively fighting to make a comeback. It has a unique and fascinating history filled with tales of Native American settlements, notorious train robberies, and rowdy railroad construction workers so prone to pulling pistols on each other that the area was nicknamed Six Shooter Siding before getting its current name in 1901. A few years later, plans for the Mother Road began, and according to local history buffs, the town prepared itself for some of the route's earliest alignments by building up its downtown accordingly. The result? Tucumcari's downtown is separated from Route 66, where most of its kitschy motels and shops are still located today.

As larger highways took over, the town was largely left behind, and examples of Tucumcari's struggles began to pop up everywhere. Many shops and motels closed their doors, but hope for a revival was not lost. Spending a day in Tucumcari means stepping back in time to Route 66's glory days.

ABOVE Del's Restaurant

Del's Restaurant
1202 E. Route 66 Blvd., Tucumcari, NM

If you find yourself in need of sustenance while in Tucumcari, there's no better place to get a good meal than Del's. It has history; a friendly, small-town atmosphere; classic, home-cooked specials; and the iconic retro signage you want from a joint in Tucumcari. If you're feeling hungry, try the chicken-fried steak or a rib eye. The enchiladas offer a real taste of New Mexico. Wash it all down with a prickly pear margarita.

Kix on 66
1102 E. Route 66 Blvd., Tucumcari, NM

For an authentic Route 66 diner experience, pull into Kix on 66, where you'll find chrome tables and classic diner grub. This place is so authentically 1950s that it's regularly used as the setting for pinup photo shoots.

ABOVE Tee Pee Curios

Tee Pee Curios
924 E. Route 66 Blvd., Tucumcari, NM

One of the last remaining curio shops in Tucumcari, Tee Pee Curios is not only awesome from the outside, but the inside is packed with all the Route 66 souvenirs, pottery, shirts, and jewelry you could ever want. Stop by after dark to check out the beautiful neon sign, one of only a few along this stretch that still light up at night.

Blue Swallow Motel
815 E. Route 66, Tucumcari, NM

The iconic Blue Swallow Motel in Tucumcari has been open since 1939. As far as vintage neon signage goes, it doesn't get much better than the Blue Swallow's classic sign. If you can, stick around until dusk; it's worth the wait. And there's a reason for the classic Tucumcari Tonite! campaign—there's no better place to stop for the night. Many rooms at the Blue Swallow come with their own garage, so you can stow your car, grab a lawn chair, and sit outside to bask in the glow of the iconic neon.

Motel Safari
722 E. Route 66 Blvd., Tucumcari, NM

Motel Safari is a fantastic motel oozing with retro charm. It's been a veritable Route 66 icon for more than 60 years. Built in 1959 by Chester Dohrer, the motel, designed in the Googie architectural style, is quite fabulous. Architecture buffs will love discovering the many details, from the excellent signage to the counter-stacked brick grids in the facade. The current owners are die-hard Route 66 enthusiasts, and they're more than happy to share a beer on the patio and tell you all about Tucumcari.

BELOW Architecture buffs will appreciate the retro Motel Safari.

Tucumcari Historical Museum
416 S. Adams St., Tucumcari, NM

The Tucumcari Historical Museum is a fantastic place to learn all about the town's history. Housed in a 1903 schoolhouse, the museum features several themed rooms and outdoor exhibits.

Mesalands Dinosaur Museum
222 E. Laughlin St., Tucumcari, NM

If you're more into prehistoric history, stop at the 10,000-square-foot dinosaur museum located in the exhibit hall of Mesalands Community College. The museum, which focuses on the Mesozoic period, is full of fossils and replicas, including a 40-foot-long torvosaurus skeleton.

Caravan Bar & Grill
1302 W. Route US 66 Blvd., Tucumcari, NM

The Caravan Bar & Grill, located at the Tristar Inn Xpress, is renowned as one of the best bars in Tucumcari. Locals and tourists alike flock here after a long day. The bartenders may not know your name when you walk in, but by night's end chances are good that you'll have made a new friend.

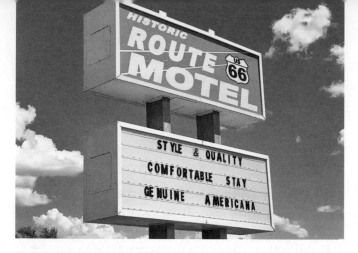

ABOVE Historic Route 66 Motel in Tucumcari *Elmar Reich/Flickr*

Extra stops

Historic Route 66 Motel *Accommodation*
1620 E. Route 66 Blvd., Tucumcari, NM

Tucumcari Ranch Supply *Shop*
502 S. Lake St., Tucumcari, NM

Watson's BBQ *Restaurant*
502 S. Lake St., Tucumcari, NM

Roadrunner Lodge Motel *Accommodation*
1023 E. Route 66 Blvd., Tucumcari, NM

Pow Wow Restaurant *Restaurant*
801 E. Route 66 Blvd., Tucumcari, NM

**Cornerstone's First Edition
Pizza & Subs** *Restaurant*
711 E. Route 66 Blvd., Tucumcari, NM

Magnolia Gas Station *Photo Op*
1016 W. Tucumcari Blvd., Tucumcari, NM

On the road . . .
Santa Rosa

Located along the Pecos River about halfway between Tucumcari and Albuquerque, the small town of Santa Rosa bustled with activity during the heyday of Route 66. Today you can visit the Route 66 Auto Museum, grab a bite to eat at the Comet II Drive-In, or take a dip in the famous Blue Hole of Santa Rosa. Alternatively known as the Scuba Diving Capital of the Southwest or the City of Natural Lakes, Santa Rosa is a desert oasis with lakes, ponds, and streams fed by natural springs.

Santa Rosa Lake State Park
NM 91, Santa Rosa, NM

The lovely Santa Rosa Lake State Park, a must-see on your journey across northeastern New Mexico, features plenty of hiking trails, ample places to camp, and numerous opportunities for water sports. Take advantage of its beautiful vistas and photo ops.

Silver Moon Cafe
2545 Historic Route 66, Santa Rosa, NM

The historical Silver Moon Cafe sits just off of Route 66 in Santa Rosa. The recently renovated restaurant

BELOW Silver Moon Cafe

has a homey feel, complete with friendly staff, reasonable prices, and a gift shop featuring Route 66 merchandise. Don't leave without trying the chips and salsa.

Blue Hole of Santa Rosa
Route 66, Santa Rosa, NM
  (near Santa Rosa Visitor Info Center, off Blue Hole Road)

Santa Rosa is probably best known for being home to the 80-foot-deep Blue Hole, a lush oasis in the middle of the desert. With crystal-clear water that remains at a perfect 62°F year-round, it's a popular place to scuba dive, or for Route 66 travelers to cool off with a dip.

BELOW Blue Hole of Santa Rosa

Santa Rosa Campground & RV Park
2136 Historic Route 66, Santa Rosa, NM

Santa Rosa Campground is a great place to spend the night after swimming in the Blue Hole. The campground has plenty of sites for both RVs and tents and offers free Wi-Fi and a heated pool. The campground is home to the Southwestern Gift Shop, which is full of authentic Native American goods and Route 66 souvenirs. The best part of the campground might just be the Western Bar-B-Q Restaurant, which offers traditional home-cooked meals delivered to your cabin or RV site.

Extra stops

Route 66 Auto Museum *Attraction*
2436 Historic Route 66, Santa Rosa, NM

Joseph's Bar & Grill *Restaurant*
1775 Route 66, Santa Rosa, NM

BELOW Route 66 Auto Museum

Greg Gjerdingen/Flickr/CC BY 2.0 (creativecommons.org/licenses/by/2.0)

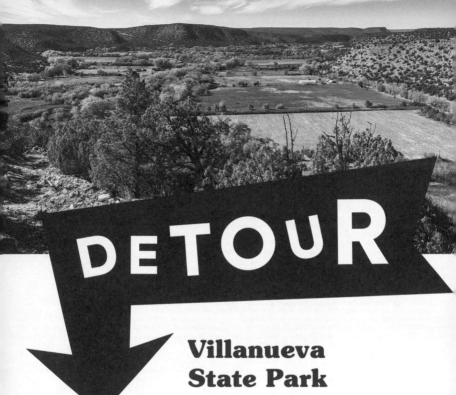

DETOUR

Villanueva State Park

135 Dodge Road, Villanueva, NM
Villanueva State Park is located between I-40 and I-25, along the Pecos River. This canyon park offers hiking trails and several sites for camping. Cell service is pretty spotty, so plan accordingly.

ABOVE Overlook at Villanueva State Park
Laurens Hoddenbagh/Shutterstock

Clines Corners Travel Center
1 Yacht Club Drive, Clines Corners, NM

Not the most economical place to gas up, but you're not stopping here for gas. You're stopping here because numerous billboards urge you to—and to explore this old-school Route 66 attraction, take a few pictures, and browse around the expansive gift shop. If you're hungry, visit the restaurant for some authentic New Mexico Green Chile.

ABOVE Clines Corners Travel Center has a gift shop and restaurant.

Wildlife West Nature Park
87 N. Frontage Road, Edgewood, NM

The Wildlife West Nature Park, which calls itself an enhanced zoo, offers an intimate wildlife preserve experience for visitors. Here you'll learn all about the special flora and fauna that make up the Southwest, and the unique ecosystems that you've been driving through. It's about 30 minutes east of Albuquerque, right off I-40.

Weirdville

The Very Large Array
Old Highway 60, 50 miles west of Socorro, NM

Imagine driving through the desert and coming across a field of massive antennas. No, you haven't entered *The Twilight Zone;* you're at the Very Large Array (VLA), the world's premier radio astronomy observatory. But what are these antennas tracking, who put them there, and why do they keep moving around?

The VLA was built in the 1970s, and a decade-long project to upgrade the equipment was finished in 2011. The array consists of 27 antennas, each with a 25-meter dish, arranged in a Y shape. The telescopes move closer together and farther apart to allow for aperture synthesis interferometry, which is basically a way to compare and learn about radio emissions from the universe beyond our own planet. Radio emissions measured by the antennas can be used to investigate anything from supernova remnants and gamma-ray

ABOVE The antennas of the Very Large Array (VLA)
Zack Frank/Shutterstock

bursts to black holes and hydrogen gas. They can even teach us about quasars, pulsars, astrophysical masers, and more.

The visitor center has a helpful film that explains exactly what the array does and how. It also offers guided and self-guided tours. Stop by around sunset for mind-blowing views.

High Country Lodge
303 First St., Magdalena, NM

If you need a place to spend the night while in the area, the High Country Lodge is located at the foot of the Magdalena Mountains. The lodge is just 5 minutes from the Boxcar Museum and some amazing hiking trails.

ABOVE Pies at The Gatherin' Place
Courtesy of The Gatherin' Place

Pie Town: The true story of a sweet town

Pie Town is a tiny town in western New Mexico known for its eponymous dessert. Founded by World War I veteran Clyde Norman in 1922, it became famous along the original Coast-to-Coast Highway for its dried fruit pies. The Great Depression took its toll on the town, but residents kept baking pies to serve the weary farmers heading west in search of opportunities. Since then, Pie Town has kept its reputation as a friendly stop where travelers can take a break from the road and enjoy a slice of home-baked pie.

The Gatherin' Place
5603 US 60, Pie Town, NM

This friendly café is one of the main pie purveyors in town. Flavors rotate daily and include peach, New Mexico apple, apricot, chocolate buttermilk, blueberry, dark chocolate and cherry, and blackberry. The 6-inch pies are served whole. They're great for splitting and pair nicely with a free cup of coffee. The café also serves up simple breakfast items such as huevos rancheros and breakfast burritos, along with green chile burgers.

Sunset Motel *Accommodation*
501 E. Old Route 66, Moriarty, NM

Whiting Bros. Service Station *Attraction*
500 Central Ave., Moriarty, NM

Crossley Park *Attraction*
SW corner of US 66 and
Howard Cavasos Blvd., Moriarty, NM

Moriarty Historical Museum *Attraction*
202 S. Broadway, Moriarty, NM

 Inside the task force that helps vintage motels
along Route 66 unite and thrive: **rt.guide/YBBX**

BELOW Whiting Bros. Service Station in Moriarty, the only Whiting Bros.
location still in operation. *Roger Holden*

184

Hollywick Farms Alpacas
503 Frost Road, Sandia Park, NM

Hollywick Farms Alpacas in Sandia Park is right along the Turquoise Trail, and it's an adorable place to stop and meet the cute couple that runs the alpaca farm. You can even feed and get little kisses from the alpacas.

Tinkertown Museum
121 Sandia Crest Road, Sandia Park, NM

Route 66 crosses the Turquoise Trail, where you can get some midcentury history in addition to the area's Native and Spanish cultural influences. Tinkertown Museum in Sandia Park is a classic roadside attraction. Ross Ward's collection of wood figures, glass bottles, and other oddities started off as a traveling exhibition at carnivals and fairs. Settling down in Sandia Park allowed Ward to expand his collection even further, adding larger items such as a 35-foot-long antique wooden sailboat that once took a 10-year voyage around the world, and Esmerelda, a fortune-telling machine.

Until recently, eastbound travelers on the desolate road between Albuquerque and Tijeras could enjoy the Singing Road, a grooved road that, when driven at exactly 45 miles per hour, played the tune of "America the Beautiful." Over the years, however, the grooves were worn down, and in June 2020, it was announced that the road would no longer be maintained.

DETOUR

National monument doubleheader

Head up I-25 to see the natural wonders at one or both of these two national monuments. Kasha-Katuwe Tent Rocks is about 50 miles north of the route, and Bandelier is about 75 miles farther. Bandelier offers first-come, first-served campsites.

Bandelier National Monument
15 Entrance Road, Los Alamos, NM
With man-made cliff dwellings dating back almost a thousand years, the 33,000-acre monument offers a glimpse at the ancient way of life. To reach the caves, follow an easy

ABOVE Bandelier National Monument   *JHVEPhoto/Shutterstock*

1.2-mile trail through Frijoles Canyon, and hike an additional mile of trail that involves climbing 140 feet via a number of stone stairs and four wooden ladders. *Note:* Using GPS to get you to the national monument is not a good plan, according to park rangers. Visit the National Park Service website for driving directions.

Kasha-Katuwe Tent Rocks National Monument

Jemez Springs Sandoval, Jemez Springs, NM

Just 40 miles west of Santa Fe, the Kasha-Katuwe Tent Rocks National Monument is home to some phenomenal slot canyons. The views from the trail are unreal—just remember to bring sunscreen and water, and wear comfortable shoes. *Note:* Your GPS may take you through tribal lands that are not accessible. Please visit the monument's website for driving directions.

BELOW Kasha-Katuwe Tent Rocks National Monument
Martina Birnbaum/Shutterstock

On the road . . .
Albuquerque

Albuquerque is a high desert city with an artsy vibe.
Admire the Pueblo architecture, explore Old Town, pop
into the Indian Pueblo Cultural Center, and learn about
the desert at the ABQ BioPark Botanic Garden.

 Known as the Flamenco Capital of North America,
Albuquerque is letting its Spanish roots shine:
rt.guide/XABU

66 Diner
1405 Central Ave. NE, Albuquerque, NM

For an authentic Route 66 meal, make a pit stop at
the 66 Diner in Albuquerque, where you can load up
on burgers, fries, strawberry shakes, and the biggest
banana split you've ever seen. The 66 Diner doesn't
just serve authentic 1950s-style food but goes out of
its way to look the part. Retro touches include chrome
tables, a jukebox loaded with period-appropriate 45
records, and waitstaff in '50s outfits. The sundaes
here are comically giant—the banana split has eight
scoops of ice cream, so get it to share.

 Albuquerque's minor league baseball team is called
the Albuquerque Isotopes, named after an episode of
The Simpsons in which Springfield's minor league team
plans to move to Albuquerque.

San Felipe de Neri Church
2005 N. Plaza St. NW, Albuquerque, NM

The San Felipe de Neri Church has been the spiritual heart of Albuquerque for more than 300 years. Built in 1793, the church is especially beautiful when it's illuminated around Christmas. It's just a quick 10–15 minutes off the highway, and the area is full of stores and restaurants, so pull over for a photo op and to stretch your legs.

Sean Pavone/Shutterstock

ABOVE San Felipe de Neri Church

DETOUR

Petroglyph National Monument

Unser Boulevard NW and Western Trail NW, Albuquerque, NM

Experience Albuquerque's Native American roots firsthand at Petroglyph National Monument, a 17-mile monument filled with an estimated 25,000 petroglyphs that can be seen from three hiking trails. The symbols give a fascinating look into another time and culture. The West Mesa volcanic escarpment is a fantastic place for hiking and discovering additional ancient rock drawings. Hit up the visitor center before embarking on your mini adventure, and have someone direct you to the best spots, such as Boca Negra Canyon.

ABOVE Petroglyphs at Petroglyph National Monument   *IrinaK/Shutterstock*

Boca Negra Canyon
Atrisco Drive NW, Albuquerque, NM

Three short hikes within the Boca Negra Canyon can be done in about an hour and put you face-to-face with more than 100 ancient petroglyphs. In fact, Petroglyph National Monument is one of the largest petroglyph sites in North America, featuring symbols carved 400–700 years ago. Bring your hiking boots. The climb can get tough and rocky, but it's totally worth the effort.

BELOW Wildflowers in Boca Negra Canyon
Steve Lagreca/Shutterstock

On the road . . .

Historic Old Town
Albuquerque, NM

Founded in 1706, Albuquerque's historic Old Town contains some of the oldest buildings in the city. Full of museums and well-preserved historic architecture, it's also home to some of the best grub in town.

BELOW Native American rugs in Old Town Albuquerque
aceshot1/Shutterstock

ABOVE Old Town Albuquerque
Doug Kerr/Flickr/CC BY-SA 2.0 (creativecommons.org/licenses/by-sa/2.0)

The Owl Cafe
800 Eubank Blvd. NE, Albuquerque, NM

The Owl Cafe is a classic diner with an eye-catching exterior (shaped like an owl), but it's the food inside that's the real star here. Home to an incredible green chile cheeseburger (a Southwest staple), the Owl Cafe offers more than 20 flavors of milkshakes, breakfast all day, and a legendary coconut cream pie. Be sure to bring extra quarters so you can spin your favorite 1950s tunes from a mini jukebox at your table.

Enchanted Trails RV Park and Trading Post
14305 Central Ave. NW, Albuquerque, NM

The Enchanted Trails park is about as scenic as a campground can get. Flanked by three extinct volcanoes, the location offers campers incredible views of the surrounding desert—especially during sunset.

American International Rattlesnake Museum

202 San Felipe St. NW, Albuquerque, NM

The American International Rattlesnake Museum will educate you on one of the Southwest's most misunderstood creatures, plus give you a good primer on what to do if you ever encounter one in the wild. The museum consists of only a few rooms, so you probably won't spend more than half an hour here unless you're lucky enough to meet Bob, the owner, who is an amazing storyteller. Come early when the snakes are especially active.

BELOW American International Rattlesnake Museum
Richie Diesterheft/Flickr/CC BY 2.0 (creativecommons.org/licenses/by-sa/2.0)

48 hours in Albuquerque

New Mexico might be the Land of Enchantment, but in Albuquerque, it's the Land of the Weird. Whether you're pondering the meaning of ancient petroglyphs, spending the night in opulent mansions, or attempting to escape from devious traps, this guide will help you explore the strangest corners of the city.

Famous for its balloon festival and association with AMC's *Breaking Bad*, this town is big on artsy Southwestern charm. Visit the National Museum of Nuclear Science & History, grab a bite to eat at Perea's New Mexican Restaurant, and tuck in for the night at the Nativo Lodge—or just drive past Walter White's house on your way through town. If you choose to stay the night, Hotel Parq Central is an old hospital turned sleek hotel, and the Casas de Suenos Old Town Historic Inn rents private casitas (cottages) in Old Town.

ABOVE Balloons at the Albuquerque International Balloon Fiesta

The Candy Lady
424 San Felipe St. NW, Albuquerque, NM

The Candy Lady has been serving up sweets to the local community for three decades, but after the producers of *Breaking Bad* came knocking, the shop suddenly became known for whipping up batches of the iconic blue "meth" used in the series.

Fortunately for us, they've continued producing it and have made it available to fans in their shop. Grab the readily available Heisenberg disguise and the staff will snap a photo of you holding the candy. If you're over 18 (and not easily offended), head to the back of the shop to see some of the most scandalous chocolate molds you've ever seen.

BaDTour
*800 Rio Grande Blvd. NW,
   Albuquerque, NM*

As the center of television's *Breaking Bad* universe, an iconic landmark from the show is always just a stone's throw away in Albuquerque. This can make coordinating your pilgrimage a little tough. Fortunately, the BaDTour from ABQ Trolley Co. will show you all the best filming locations, including the hard-to-find hidden secrets. The best part? They do the driving.

Bottger Mansion
Bed and Breakfast
*110 San Felipe St. NW,
   Albuquerque, NM*

The Bottger Mansion Bed and Breakfast, located in historic Old Town, features photographs, antiques, and memorabilia dating back to the arrival of the railroad in 1879. It also has all the modern amenities. The guest rooms, all named for prominent Albuquerqueans, come decorated and furnished with biographies and historical photos (so you'll know the exact identity of the ghost that comes to haunt you later in the evening). Be sure to book your reservation well in advance. This is one of the best bed and breakfasts in the city and it fills up fast.

Monte Carlo Steakhouse and Liquor Store
3916 Central Ave. SW, Albuquerque, NM

At the Monte Carlo Steakhouse and Liquor Store, you can order some of the best prime cuts in the state and grab a bottle of your favorite spirit while you wait. The prime rib is available only after 5 p.m., so plan accordingly. Wondering about the wine selection? The restaurant is attached to a liquor store, so pick any wine in the store and they'll bring it to your table.

The National Museum of Nuclear Science & History
601 Eubank Blvd. SE, Albuquerque, NM

Get ready to learn everything you never knew you wanted to know about the benefits—and dangers—of nuclear energy. The National Museum of Nuclear Science & History houses an amazing collection of artifacts, from full-size Cold War–era aircraft to miniature models of nuclear power plants. Many of the tour guides are retired military personnel with hands-on experience working with nuclear science, so don't be afraid to ask questions.

Walter White's Final Resting Place
6855 Fourth St., Los Ranchos de
   Albuquerque, NM

Pay your respects to *Breaking Bad*'s antihero with a
visit to Walter White's final resting place. This headstone was erected a few years back as a way of giving
fans a little extra closure. The headstone can be a bit
tough to find, but poke around the back of the strip
mall and you'll discover it mounted to the wall.

Anderson-Abruzzo Albuquerque International Balloon Museum
9201 Balloon Museum Drive NE,
   Albuquerque, NM

The Anderson-Abruzzo Albuquerque International
Balloon Museum, designed to look like a hot-air
balloon resting on its side, houses artifacts that tell
the history of balloon excursions, from crossing the
Atlantic Ocean to crossing the planet. Never been
on a hot-air balloon ride? You can try out the simu-
lator and decide whether the heights are for you. If
you visit during October, you'll be able to catch the
awe-inspiring sights of the Albuquerque International
Balloon Fiesta, when hundreds of hot-air balloons fill
the skies above the city.

Tamaya Mist in the Hyatt Regency Tamaya Resort and Spa
1300 Tuyuna Trail, Santa Ana Pueblo, NM

The Tamaya Mist spa in the Hyatt Regency Tamaya
Resort and Spa offers visitors a unique relaxation
experience. The ancient drumming treatment features
a full-body rubdown made with mud from the Jemez
Mountains infused with red chile, which the resort
says will detoxify your body. If that doesn't do the
trick, the spa's relaxation room is fully stocked with
green chile–infused granola and red chile chocolate.

Is it true that the breakfast burrito originated in the 1970s at the Albuquerque International Balloon Fiesta? No one really knows, but we love a good origin story.

Extra stops

May Cafe *Restaurant*
111 Louisiana Blvd. SE, Albuquerque, NM

Absolutely Neon *Shop*
3903 Central Ave. NE, Albuquerque, NM

Nob Hill *Neighborhood*
Central Ave., Albuquerque, NM

KiMo Theatre *Attraction*
423 Central Ave. NW, Albuquerque, NM

Dog House Drive In *Restaurant*
1216 Central Ave. NW, Albuquerque, NM

SPOTLIGHT

The Breaking Bad Guide to ABQ

The final episode of *Breaking Bad* may have aired in 2013, but the show's impact on Albuquerque is still obvious. Bakeries selling "blue meth" donuts, packets of crystal-blue rock sugar, and a beauty salon with a line of Bathing Bad bath salts are just a few of the themed treats you can find while exploring the city.

For a place that was once mostly known for its annual Balloon Fiesta, the dark and violent nature of the series hasn't stopped Albuquerque, or its residents, from embracing all the attention it's brought to the city. What better way for fans to reminisce about Walter White's journey than to follow in the character's footsteps on this *Breaking Bad* side trip? Here's our guide to the most iconic filming locations. Just remember to tread lightly.

ABOVE Crossroads Motel (see page 202)
Pom'/Flickr/CC BY-SA 2.0 (creativecommons.org/licenses/by-sa/2.0)

Walter White's House
3828 Piermont Drive, Albuquerque, NM

Generally speaking, standing outside Walter White's (aka Heisenberg's) house and snapping pictures is probably a bad idea; in Heisenberg's Albuquerque, you might find yourself dissolving in a plastic barrel, but lucky for us, it's not as dangerous in real life. Frances Padilla had no idea what she was getting herself into when she agreed to let her home of 40 years become the fictional residence of the turbulent White family. On a monthly basis, hundreds of fans pull up to her curb and pile out to take pictures of themselves in sunglasses and black bowler hats.

Mister Car Wash
(formerly Octopus Car Wash)
9516 Snow Heights Circle NE, Albuquerque, NM

Breaking Bad singlehandedly turned a perfectly harmless car wash into one of the seediest places in the U.S. Walt and Skyler might have been using their A1A car wash to clean a whole lot of dirty cash, but its real-life counterpart, Mister Car Wash, focuses primarily on washing cars. You can pull in for a wash or just snap some photos, as it's open to the general public. Tell 'em Walt sent you.

Delta Uniform & Linen
1617 Candelaria Road NE, Albuquerque, NM

There might not be a superlab located deep in the basement of this laundry facility, but you can still visit Delta Uniform & Linen, the location that set the stage for so many tense moments between Heisenberg and Fring in season four.

Pinkman Residence
322 16th St., Albuquerque, NM

Hydrofluoric acid and a body in a bathtub: welcome to Jesse Pinkman's (first) home. The location of Pinkman's fictional home changed some time during production of the second season, when the original homeowners sold the property, but if you pop over to 16th Street, you can see both in one easy trip. Just remember to be respectful since these are private residences.

Java Joe's
906 Park Ave. SW, Albuquerque, NM

Tuco's headquarters has a distinctive look in the show. In real life, it's a local coffee shop called Java Joe's that serves up great breakfast food, baked goods, and live music.

Crossroads Motel
1001 Central Ave. NE, Albuquerque, NM

Nicknamed The Crystal Palace, the Crossroads Motel was featured in a musical montage that had everyone humming "Everyone Knows It's Windy" the next day. Though the motel stopped making appearances in later seasons, it's an iconic part of *Breaking Bad*'s imagery and well worth a visit.

Ace Metals Inc.
5711 Broadway Blvd. SE, Albuquerque, NM

A handful of separate locations were used to make up Joe's Salvage throughout the series, but only one bore witness to the end of the RV: Ace Metals. Stop by to pay your respects to the rolling meth lab and yell, "Yeah, bitch! Magnets!"

Twisters Burgers and Burritos
4275 Isleta Blvd., Albuquerque, NM

Jose La Rivera, manager of the South Valley burrito joint that served as the set of the series' famous Los Pollos Hermanos restaurant, says that up to 40 fans a day come—sometimes straight from the airport—in search of *Breaking Bad's* Gus Fring. The show's popularity has been great for La Rivera, who says that fan interest in the restaurant has brought in new customers excited to sit in the most coveted seat in the place: Walt's booth. Ask La Rivera to snap your photo next to the huge Los Pollos Hermanos mural.

To'hajiilee Indian Reservation
Bernalillo West, NM

To'hajiilee Indian Reservation is the perfect starting and ending point for a *Breaking Bad* side trip, playing an important role in both the beginning and end of Walt's journey. The first place Walt and Jesse parked the rolling meth lab, it was also prominently featured at the climax of the series. Formerly known as the Canoncito Reservation, To'hajiilee is a section of the Navajo Nation between three of New Mexico's southwestern counties. The dry, rocky terrain has a certain desolate beauty.

ABOVE "Blue Meth" candy at The Candy Lady (see page 195)
Pom'/Flickr/CC BY-SA 2.0 (creativecommons.org/licenses/by-sa/2.0)

You're more than halfway through, but don't get nostalgic just yet; there's still plenty left to see on your way into Arizona.

The trading posts—and opportunities to buy moccasins—will become more frequent as you head farther into the desert Southwest. Grants, Gallup, and Holbrook are all historic towns full of top-notch neon and whimsical motels, so take your time and enjoy the dry air and colorful sunsets.

Keep an eye out for black rocks that line the road between Grants and Gallup, as this part of the route follows the Zuni-Bandera Volcanic Field.

Leg 5: Albuquerque to Flagstaff

335 Miles

Find a complete Online Trip Guide for leg 5:

rt.guide/TGNC

Standin' on the Corner Park
Winslow, AZ

Meteor Crater
Winslow, AZ

04

Albuquerque
New Mexico

06 **05** **02** **01**

Flagstaff
Arizona

Petrified Forest National Park
Arizona

03

Wigwam Village Motel No. 6
Holbrook, AZ

Leg 5: Albuquerque to Flagstaff

Route highlights

01 Albuquerque

Petrified Forest National Park **02**

03 Wigwam Village Motel No. 6

Standin' on the Corner Park **04**

05 Meteor Crater

Flagstaff **06**

Featured campgrounds

Holbrook/Petrified Forest KOA
102 Hermosa Drive, Holbrook, AZ

This is a great base camp for exploring the Painted Desert and Petrified Forest National Park. It's also just an hour west of Meteor Crater. The campground offers full-hookup RV sites, tent sites, and cabins.

Flagstaff KOA
5803 N. US 89, Flagstaff, AZ

This KOA has standard RV and tenting accommodations, as well as tepees and deluxe cabins. The scenic campground is full of ponderosa pines, and is located less than an hour from the Red Rocks of Sedona.

Featured accommodations

Wigwam Village Motel No. 6
811 W. Hopi Drive, Holbrook, AZ

If you are going to stay in just one Wigwam Village during your Route 66 adventure, this is the one to choose. It's listed on the National Register of Historic Places, and each wigwam features a full bathroom, air conditioning, and cable television. The motel is open year-round, and reservations can be made up to six months in advance at reserveamerica.com. (Also see page 228.)

Enchanted Trails RV Park & Trading Post
14305 Central Ave. NW, Albuquerque, NM

Located directly on historic Route 66, the Enchanted Trails RV Park & Trading Post is only minutes from Petroglyph National Monument and Volcanoes Day Use Area. There is also a charming collection of vintage RVs on-site, providing additional Route 66 vibes and photo ops.

Playlist
Listen here: rt.guide/RZMW

Songs to get you in the mood while on the road . . .

1. "New Mexico," Nevada Color

2. "Maria Elena," New Mexico–the Sound of Enchantment

3. "The Crooked Trail to Holbrook," Slim Critchlow

4. "Arizona," Kings of Leon

5. "Get Back," The Beatles

6. "Mesa Town," Authority Zero

7. "Tune Out," The Format

8. "Take It Easy," the Eagles

9. "Readymade," Red Hot Chili Peppers

On the road . . .
New Mexico

Today, the New Mexico section of Route 66 clocks in at just over 250 miles of remaining road, but that wasn't always the case. The original alignment, mapped out in 1926, covered more than 500 miles through the Land of Enchantment and included an S-shaped detour in the middle of the state. When the New Mexico portion of the route was redrawn in 1937, more than 100 miles were knocked off.

On the road . . .
Albuquerque

Laguna Pueblo
45 minutes west of Albuquerque,
right on Route 66

When you pass the whitewashed St. Joseph's Church, you'll know that you've arrived at the Laguna Pueblo, which spans four counties and is made up of six villages. Part of the pueblo dates back to the 1400s, but people have been settled in the area since at least the 1300s, and tribes have passed through since 3000 B.C. The pueblo is especially fun to visit during feast days: March 19, July 25–26, August 10, August 15, September 8, September 19, September 25, and October 17.

ABOVE View of the New Mexican landscape from Route 66 between Gallup and Arizona   *Gimas/Shutterstock*

**Mission San José de Laguna
(St. Joseph's Church)** *Attraction*
1 Friar Road, New Laguna, NM

Budville Trading Co. *Attraction*
Old Route 66, Casa Blanca, NM

Villa de Cubero Trading Post *Shop*
1406 NM 124, Casa Blanca, NM

St. Joseph's Mission School *Attraction*
26 School Road, San Fidel, NM

San Estevan del Rey Mission Church
Attraction South of I-40 on NM 23
at Acoma Pueblo, NM

Santa Maria de Acoma Church *Attraction*
Main Road, McCartys, NM

New Mexico Mining Museum
100 Iron Ave., Grants, NM

There should always be room in your itinerary for one more mining museum. At this one, you'll learn all about the "carrot capital" of the U.S. Grants, which began as a logging town in the 1880s, suffered during the 1930s as the industry declined. The town took advantage of its volcanic soils, which were quite fertile, and turned to agriculture to revitalize the local economy. But it was the discovery of uranium near Haystack Mesa by a Navajo shepherd that really created a boom. The mining boom lasted until the late 1980s, when the town once again sank into an economic depression. Today, Grants sees a steady stream of tourists and is a great place to stop for vintage motels and neon-sign photo ops.

DE**TOU**R

Ice Cave and Bandera Volcano

12000 Ice Caves Road, Grants, NM
The Ice Cave and Bandera Volcano, south of Grants, is a privately owned and operated cave, absolutely worth its $6–$12 entrance fee. There's a half-mile walk to the volcano and a 400-yard walk to the Ice Cave, which, thanks to

ABOVE Sunlight illuminates natural algae, giving the ice its greenish color.
Jon Manjeot/Shutterstock

ABOVE Bandera Volcano
Henryk Sadura/Shutterstock

its low temperatures, creates green ice forma-
tions that are around 20 feet thick. Be sure to
wear good shoes because the trail is lined with
tiny pebbles and can be difficult to traverse
without good traction. If you visit in the hot
summer months, this stop can be a cool and
refreshing break from the road.

DETOUR

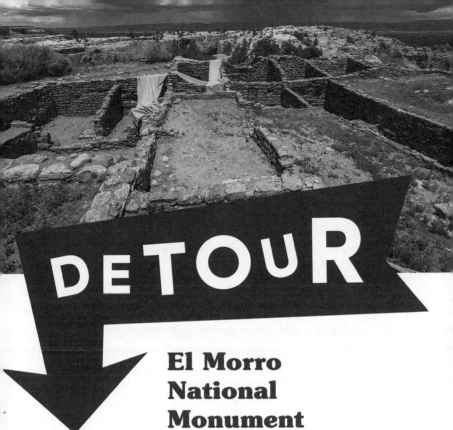

DETOUR

El Morro National Monument

Ramah, NM

At El Morro National Monument, you can read messages that ancient Puebloan, Spanish, and American travelers carved into the sandstone over hundreds of years. Plan to stop for a minimum of 30 minutes to see the base of the monument and if you have time, take a 2-mile round-trip hike to the top to see what remains of the ancestral Puebloan dwellings. Note that the trail is closed periodically throughout the day, so it's best to arrive at least a few hours before closing.

ABOVE Ruins of the ancestral pueblo of Atsinna at El Morro
Jon Manjeot/Shutterstock

Wow Diner
1300 Motel Drive, Milan, NM

The Wow Diner will make you feel as if you've traveled back in time to the 1950s. This is a popular spot, so prepare for a wait. Order one of the homemade milkshakes, made with real ice cream, or a glass of wine or beer—something you don't always find at retro diners.

Bowlin's Old Crater Trading Post
7650 Frontage Road (Old Route 66), Bluewater, NM

Bowlin's Old Crater Trading Post, named after the volcanic crater nearby, was built in 1954 by Claude Bowlin, replacing an earlier post at the same location that was built in 1936. Bowlin's closed in 1973 after I-40 bypassed the town, but it has since been added to the National Register of Historic Places. The trading post is permanently closed—and the interior isn't accessible—but it's a great photo op.

Extra stops

Red Mountain Market & Deli
Abandoned Attraction
NM 122 (US Route 66) at NM 371, Thoreau, NM

Roy T. Herman's Garage and Service Station *Attraction*
NM 122, 150 yards west of I-40
Exit 53 in Thoreau, NM

Red Rock Park *Attraction*
825 Outlaw Road, Church Rock, NM

On the road . . .
Gallup

Gallup is the largest city between Albuquerque and Flagstaff along Route 66, and it's full of motels, dining options, and neon signage. Because it lies in the middle of a Navajo reservation, you'll also find an abundance of Native American crafts, artwork, and history. Don't miss the Muffler Man cowboy just off the route near downtown, and if you're staying overnight, you can't beat the Old Hollywood–style El Rancho Hotel.

El Rancho Hotel
1000 E. US 66, Gallup, NM

This historic, Western-style hotel was built by Joe Massaglia in 1936 and has been featured in dozens of Old Hollywood movies. It is listed on the National Register of Historic Places and features wagon-wheel headboards and suites named after famous Hollywood Western stars. Even if you don't spend the night here,

ABOVE Stay overnight or just stop for lunch at El Rancho Hotel.

at least pull over to check out the epic hunting lodge–inspired lobby, which is full of antiques and Native American decor. The on-site restaurant makes a delicious green chile enchilada, a tasty margarita, and the crispiest pancakes you'll find along the route.

USA RV Park
2925 W. Historic US 66, Gallup, NM

One reason Route 66 became so popular is because it crosses some of the country's most unique landscapes. The USA RV Park, located just off the historic route, is a great place to soak up some of those old-school road trip vibes. With a nightly cookout (May–October), a multitude of activities, and well-kept facilities, this spot is a great reminder of why road trips are so much fun.

Extra Stops

El Morro Theatre *Attraction*
207 W. Coal Ave., Gallup, NM

Rex Museum *Attraction*
300 W. Historic US 66, Gallup, NM

Muffler Man Cowboy at John's Used Cars
Attraction
416 W. Coal Ave., Gallup, NM

The Continental Divide National Scenic Trail crosses Route 66 in a small village named—you guessed it—Continental Divide, New Mexico.

On the road...
Arizona

You'll know you're crossing into Arizona when you spot the large, bright-white Teepee Trading Post advertising jewelry, pottery, kachinas, and Southwestern souvenirs. The teepee-shaped souvenir shop is set against a striking backdrop of dramatic red-rock cliffs, and it's a great place to pull over, grab a drink, and load up on souvenirs. With the exception of the Navajo Nation, most of Arizona does not observe Daylight Saving Time, so be sure to confirm the time as you cross the Arizona–New Mexico border.

Chief Yellowhorse Trading Post
359 I-40, Lupton, AZ

Once you enter Arizona, Yellowhorse Trading Post, conveniently located on I-40 in Lupton (and next to the Teepee Trading Post), should be your first stop. This Navajo-owned trading post has been run by the Yellowhorse family since the 1950s, when they began selling Navajo rugs and petrified wood to travelers.

ABOVE Route 66 sign in Arizona

ABOVE Chief Yellowhorse Trading Post

Allentown Bridge
Puerco River, Houck, AZ

The Allentown Bridge, located in Apache County, is a great photo op. Built in 1923, the bridge crosses the Puerco River and is on the National Register of Historic Places. While you're in the neighborhood, the Querino Canyon Bridge on old Route 66, just a few miles away, is another stunner.

Hubbell Trading Post
0.5 mile west of AZ 264, Ganado, AZ

The historic Hubbell Trading Post in Ganado is the oldest operating trading post in the Navajo Nation. It is also a testament to the impact of Navajo culture, history, and traditions in the Southwest.

DETOUR

Petrified Forest National Park

1 Park Road, Petrified Forest, AZ

A forest in the middle of Arizona's grassland may sound odd, but Petrified Forest National Park is unlike any other forest in the country. The park is packed with gems—quite literally, as the ancient wood has been turned into sparkly stone—that anyone, from outdoor enthusiasts to science geeks, can enjoy.

The park's location right off the highway means that many people at least drive through it (though it closes as early as 5 p.m.). A portion of old Route 66 is located within the park—the only portion of the classic road to still be preserved within a national park (the asphalt is gone, so it's not drivable, but look for the old

ABOVE Petrified logs   *Paul B. Moore/Shutterstock*

telephone poles marking the route). Wilderness camping is available within the park, and there are plans for a campground in 2021. Homolovi State Park, about an hour away, also offers camping. Nearby Holbrook offers additional accommodation and camping options, including a KOA.

Don't let the glittering logs tempt you into snagging a souvenir—removing any petrified wood from the park is illegal. You can purchase a box of petrified wood from a gift store

BELOW Painted Desert Visitor Center

DETOUR

(sourced from private lands), but don't open it until you've left the park premises.

Summers in the park can get hot, with little to offer in the way of shade, and winters are often cold and snowy. Wildflowers pop up throughout the desert between March and October, especially in May, July, and August, so if you're looking for an extra-colorful land-scape, this is a good time to visit.

Painted Desert Visitor Center

The Painted Desert Visitor Center is a good first stop on your tour of the park. It has an educa-tional film, a gift shop, and plenty of petrified wood for sale.

Painted Desert Inn

The national park is home to the famous Painted Desert Inn, and even though you can't spend the night here anymore, you should defi-nitely stop in to check out the exhibits (the inn was originally constructed of petrified wood, until a makeover in the 1930s). Don't miss the displays of artwork from the park's resident artist program.

Kachina Point

For the best views—and to see how the Painted Desert got its name—head to Kachina Point. Bands of different-colored sediment in the roll-ing hills make for a perfect photo op.

Puerco Pueblo

There's more to Petrified Forest National Park than its eponymous sparkly logs; it's also an important archaeological and anthropological site. Visitors can still check out the sandstone ruins of Puerco Pueblo, a once-bustling com-munity dating back to the 1200s.

Near Puerco Pueblo you'll find a spiral petroglyph on a boulder that aligns perfectly with a beam of sunlight for about two weeks near the solstice. The shaft of sunlight travels down the side of the spiral and touches the center as the sun rises, peaking at 9 a.m. If you happen to be visiting outside of the two-week window, you can still see the boulder and read the informative sign nearby.

Rainbow Forest Museum

Inside the national park, tour the Rainbow Forest Museum featuring hands-on exhibits and displays. Behind the museum is one of Petrified Forest's best hikes, the Giant Logs Trail. If you're limited on time and looking to get as much out of the park as possible, this is a great place to start.

Rainbow Forest

Watching educational videos and looking at displays is a good way to get background on the petrified wood, but nothing beats seeing the actual thing up close. It's a surprising experience to see so many sparkly, colorful logs in one place, and it's hard to believe that these trees are 220 million years old.

Agate House

The eight-room Agate House was likely built between the years 1050 and 1300 and was reconstructed in the 1930s. It was built using petrified wood and is still in remarkably good condition. See it for yourself by hiking the 2-mile round-trip trail from the Rainbow Forest visitor center.

DETOUR

Crystal Forest

The Crystal Forest is an easy hike along a paved walkway. The loop, named for the quartz crystals sometimes found in the wood, takes you past piles of petrified wood. It's only 0.75 mile, but take your time and enjoy the views.

Blue Mesa Trail

The 1-mile Blue Mesa Trail takes you farther into the Painted Desert, where the hills take on hues of gray, purple, and blue. It's definitely not a typical desert landscape—seriously, it looks like you're on a different planet—which makes it well worth a visit.

Newspaper Rock

For a park that's less than 150 square miles in size, it's pretty impressive that more than 600 archaeological sites have been found within Petrified Forest's boundaries. The cryptic petroglyphs on Newspaper Rock were carved between 650 and 2,000 years ago. Visit and try to decipher their meanings.

 The next time you visit a national park, take time to learn and honor its Indigenous history: **rt.guide/JXFZ**

On the road . . .
Holbrook

Holbrook is a town that has defied extinction, in more ways than one. It's one of the rare Route 66 towns that managed to scrape by after the Mother Road was decommissioned. Holbrook is steeped in retro vibes and remains filled with touristy kitsch, and its proximity to Petrified Forest National Park hasn't hurt its popularity. Whether you're trying to find the best deal on gemstones and souvenirs or you're in search of as many dinosaur statues as possible, Holbrook is worth exploring. It also happens to be home to the iconic Wigwam Village Motel No. 6, so you can spend the night and grab a breakfast burrito smothered in red or green chile from Joe and Aggie's Cafe in the morning.

Holbrook is located in an area filled with fossils from the Triassic Period, which ended more than 200 million years ago; the national park's signature petrified wood is just one incredible example. The remains of extinct beasts such as the phytosaur and allokotosaur have been found here as well.

Stewart's Petrified Wood
9406 Washboard Road, Holbrook, AZ

At Stewart's Petrified Wood, you can buy the world's most colorful petrified wood—some of which the store claims is more than 225 million years old.

BELOW Stewart's Petrified Wood

The dinosaurs of Holbrook

Although dinosaurs no longer roam the earth, you'll still find plenty in Holbrook. Most of the town's statues came from its International Petrified Forest and Painted Desert, the suspiciously familiar name of a former roadside attraction. When it closed in 2007, many of the dinosaur statues were relocated to various rock shops and tourist attractions in Holbrook, such as Jim Gray's Petrified Wood Co. and the Hopi Travel Plaza.

Today, the largest collection of dinosaurs stands in front of the Rainbow Rock Shop, but it didn't come from the International Petrified Forest. The owner of the shop built the seven concrete dinosaurs himself over 20 years. If you catch the owners while the shop is open, they may charge you to pose for photos with their herd; otherwise you can snap photos for free from the sidewalk.

Across Hopi Drive, the bronze dinosaur was donated to the town by a wealthy Arizona family who purchased the piece with the intention of turning it into a shower for their outdoor pool. When that didn't work out, Holbrook acquired yet another piece for its collection.

Joe and Aggie's Cafe
120 W. Hopi Drive, Holbrook, AZ

This classic Route 66 restaurant is best known for its homemade red and green chile sauces. Even if you're not hungry, it's worth stopping for a photo in front of the building, which features a hand-painted map of Route 66 (pictured above).

Wigwam Village Motel No. 6
811 W. Hopi Drive, Holbrook, AZ

Drive through the Painted Desert and Petrified Forest National Park in the late afternoon, and then stop at Wigwam Village Motel No. 6 for the night. The rooms of this charming historic motel—located inside individual concrete and steel teepees—are pure road-side kitsch. There are only three remaining Wigwam Motels, and the vintage cars parked outside of each room make this the best one for photos. (Also see page 210.)

The remaining three Wigwam Village Motels are located in Holbrook, Arizona; Cave City, Kentucky; and Rialto/San Bernardino, California.

ABOVE Wigwam Village Motel No. 6

Globetrotter Lodge
902 W. Hopi Drive, Holbrook, AZ

If the Wigwam motel is full, head across Route 66 to the Globetrotter Lodge. This classic motel features 10 adorable, cozy rooms with ample parking space for trailers or large RVs.

World's Largest Petrified Tree at Geronimo Trading Post
5372 Geronimo Road, Holbrook, AZ

We don't know for sure that this is actually the world's largest petrified tree, but it is definitely big, reportedly weighing 80 tons. Stop for a photo, do a little climbing, and then it's on to the next stop.

Aliberto's Mexican Food
1440 Navajo Blvd., Holbrook, AZ

When you're ready for a bite to eat, head to Aliberto's, a local chain that serves up authentic Mexican cuisine. If you order only one dish while in Holbrook, make it the green chile plate from Aliberto's—green chile (spelled with an *e*) is a local specialty, and after eating here you'll understand why it's so popular.

Extra stops

Hopi Travel Plaza *Shop*
1851 AZ 77, Holbrook, AZ

Navajo County Historical Society *Attraction*
100 E. Arizona St., Holbrook, AZ

Jack Rabbit Trading Post *Shop*
3386 US 66, Joseph City, AZ

BELOW Ruins at Homolovi State Park

ABOVE Homolovi State Park entrance

Homolovi State Park
AZ 87, Winslow, AZ

Homolovi State Park is home to 13th- and 14th-century artifacts and ruins. The park offers year-round petroglyph tours, a museum, and trails leading to the beautiful ruins. There is also overnight camping with electricity, water, and clean shower facilities. Homolovi is the closest campground to Petrified Forest National Park.

"Take it Easy," written by Jackson Browne and Glenn Frey, was a big hit for the Eagles, but it may have been an even bigger hit for the town of Winslow, Arizona. Like so many other Route 66 towns, Winslow was bypassed when I-40 came rolling through the Southwest. The main streets of town, once filled with travelers, were suddenly empty. But today, tourists have returned, thanks in large part to Browne, Frey, and their catchy lyrics: "Well I'm a-standin' on a corner in Winslow, Arizona, and such a fine sight to see. It's a girl, my Lord, in a flatbed Ford, slowin' down to take a look at me."

One of the best things about Winslow is the friendly locals—some will even stop their cars to avoid ruining your photo op at the Standin' on the Corner Park. You can hang out with them at the Sipp Shoppe, a coffee shop and ice-cream parlor across the street from the park.

Standin' on the Corner Park
N. Kinsley Ave. and W. Second St.

Thanks to this park, Winslow is back on the map as tourists once again travel through the heart of town. The park features a couple of statues and a mural of a girl in a red Ford truck, with the flatbed perpetually parked across the street. But this perfect photo op is only the beginning of what Winslow has to offer.

La Posada Hotel
303 E. Second St.

The resurgence of Winslow didn't start entirely on the corner. During the town's heyday as a stop for steam locomotives, hotelier Fred Harvey wanted to build a landmark hotel there. With a price tag that would equal nearly $40 million today, La Posada Hotel was completed just after the stock market crash. It would be open for only 27 years, eventually having most of its fine furnishings sold at auction, but efforts to save the Winslow icon finally succeeded.

After facing the threat of demolition for several decades, the property was finally restored by the La Posada Foundation and the hotel's new owners to its former glory as the Jewel of the West. The foundation changed its name to the Standin' on the Corner Foundation and took on its next project, helping to make the now-famous park a reality.

BELOW Standin' on the Corner Park   *Fred LaBounty/Shutterstock*

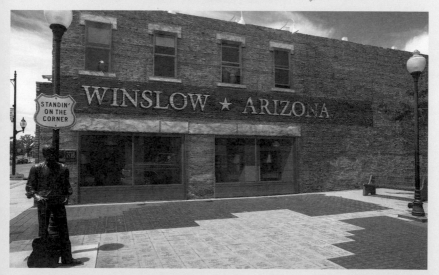

The Turquoise Room
303 E. Second St., Winslow, AZ

The Turquoise Room is a hidden gem located inside La Posada Hotel. It's a refreshingly different experience from the many diners and fast food joints that line the highway. Here you can sit down and enjoy a nice meal that feels like something you might find in a big city, with an Arizona twist.

Rock Art Ranch
Rock Art Ranch Road, Winslow, AZ

Rock Art Ranch is a privately owned working cattle ranch that was originally a part of the Hashknife Cattle Co. It's also home to incredible Anasazi dwellings and petroglyphs, and the on-site museum is a labor of love by proprietor Brantley Baird.

Extra stops

9/11 Remembrance Garden *Attraction*
E. Third St. and Transcon Lane, Winslow, AZ

Whiting Bros. Gas Station *Attraction*
Bales Ave. and E. Second St., Winslow, AZ

Old Trails Museum *Attraction*
212 N. Kinsley Ave., Winslow, AZ

Route 66 Delta Motel *Accommodation*
2141 W. Third St., Winslow, AZ

Weirdville

The Mogollon Monster

The Mogollon Monster of the Mogollon Rim in central and eastern Arizona is—allegedly—a nocturnal, omnivorous, bipedal humanoid that stands more than 7 feet tall and is covered in long, ragged hair. Mogollon Monster sightings have been reported since the early 1900s, and it's often described as a creature similar to Bigfoot, smelling of dead fish. Those obsessed with the Mogollon Monster claim they have found hair samples, footprints, and photo and video evidence. However, scientists have never found conclusive proof of its existence. If you do venture out to the Mogollon Rim for a quiet camping trip, don't be shocked if the wildlife sounds you hear are actually the monster—it reportedly mimics the sounds of birds and coyotes. Over the years it has been sighted wandering the ponderosa pine forests near Heber; in Prescott; near the Fort Apache Indian Reservation; and around Clifton and Payson.

Meteor Crater
I-40 Exit 233, Winslow, AZ

Just outside of Flagstaff is one of the weirdest attractions in the West: Meteor Crater. The impact crater formed when a meteor hit Earth about 50,000 years ago and left a massive, almost mile-wide hole in the ground. The visitor center features a museum, videos, and a great observation deck.

BELOW Meteor crater in Winslow, Arizona
Eleri Denham/Shutterstock

Two Guns is located 30 miles east of Flagstaff, on the rim of Canyon Diablo. Legend has it that in 1878, Two Guns was the site of a mass murder. Apaches hid from their Navajo enemies inside a cave; when a fire was lit at the cave's entrance, 42 people were asphyxiated inside. The cave, now called the Apache Death Cave, is still accessible by a rickety wooden ladder.

In 1922, Earle and Louise Cundiff purchased the land and built a store, restaurant, and gas station. Three years later, Harry Miller leased the property from the Cundiffs; added a zoo, gift shop, and post office; and began offering tours of the cave. In 1926, the highway that passed by Two Guns was renamed Route 66—and Miller shot and killed Cundiff during an argument (Cundiff was unarmed, but Miller was acquitted).

In the late '60s, a motel, a tavern, new zoo exhibits, a Shell service station, and a KOA campground were added to the site. The service station burned in 1971, and the site has sat abandoned ever since. The buildings are in various states of ruin, and the kidney-shaped swimming pool is covered in colorful graffiti, making it a great place for photos. There are rumors that the site also contains buried treasure and more than one dead body. While we can neither confirm nor deny these claims, you might want to bring a metal detector just in case.

On the road . . .
Sedona

Sedona is one of those places you just have to experience in person; even the most spectacular photos don't fully do it justice. Surrounded by majestic red-rock canyons and pine forests, this small desert town is known for its vibrant art scene and mysterious healing forces. Yes, you read that right—Sedona is supposedly a hotbed of cosmic activity, sitting atop several energy vortexes that are easily accessible through hikes and tours. With its artsy vibe and comfortable climate, Sedona is also home to cute shops and restaurants, galleries, and lots of aging hippies.

DETOUR

Exploring the ancient mysteries of Sedona

Montezuma Castle National Monument
2800 Montezuma Castle Highway,
Camp Verde, AZ

Montezuma Castle National Monument might be one of the greatest misnomers in the country.

ABOVE Montezuma Castle National Monument
noiseshapes/Shutterstock

It looks nothing like a castle, never housed kings or knights, and was built well before Aztec warlord Montezuma was even born. So if Montezuma Castle wasn't used as a castle and Montezuma never lived there, how did it get its name?

When American settlers first encountered the ruins in the 1860s, they mistakenly assumed it was built by, and for, the Aztec emperor. In reality, the crumbling building was actually more of an apartment complex for the Sinagua people and built between 1100 and 1425. It was mostly abandoned (empty of residents but frequently visited by Indigenous people as well as looters) about 40 years before Montezuma was born.

Now it's known that the Sinaguas built the dwelling to avoid having their homes destroyed when Beaver Creek, which provided necessary water for their crops, flooded each year. That way they could continue farming while having their homes above the ground, where the water couldn't touch them. The complex grew to be about 4,000 square feet spread across five stories, perched perilously on the side of a cliff.

Against seemingly impossible odds, the structure is still intact today, a testament to the Sinaguas' engineering and construction skills. After the people left, the "castle" sat mostly abandoned until it was declared a national monument through the American Antiquities Act of 1906. You can't go inside anymore, but you can get pretty close.

Oak Creek Canyon
AZ 89A, Sedona, AZ

Sedona's Oak Creek Canyon Scenic Drive is a little slice of desert paradise filled with churches, hiking trails, jewelry, and more. Make a quick stop at the Oak Creek Canyon Vista. Here, you can soak up the views of Sedona and browse Native American jewelry and crafts. The Airport Mesa hiking trail offers more than just breathtaking views of red rocks, stately pines, and majestic mesas—you'll also get to visit a vortex.

Sedona is known for being home to more than one site of swirling energy said to have an effect on one's mental or spiritual self. People who come to Sedona to visit one of four vortexes usually spend time meditating, praying, or reflecting at the sites. Whether you're a

DETOUR

ABOVE Cathedral Rock over Oak Creek Canyon
Nicholas Peter Gavin Davies/Shutterstock

staunch believer in the power of an energy vortex or just a curious observer, these are definitely worth a visit.

After you've been reenergized by the vortex or the scenery, check out the Chapel of the Holy Cross for a more traditional spiritual experience. This Catholic church was built right into a rocky mesa by a local rancher and artist so people of all religions and creeds could have a place to reflect on Sedona's beauty. And if you're feeling extra inspired, you won't be surprised to learn that it is also built on the alleged site of another Sedona vortex.

Pink Jeep Tours
204 N. AZ 89A, Sedona, AZ

To really get a feel for Sedona, go off-road. Pink Jeep Tours has been operating tours of the Sedona outback for more than half a century. Popular tours include the Ancient Ruin and Broken Arrow tours.

BELOW Pink Jeep Tours

mroach/Flickr/CC BY-SA 2.0 (creativecommons.org/licenses/by-sa/2.0)

There's only one more section of the Mother Road left to complete—and while we don't want to play favorites and say we saved the best for last, there are still plenty of roadside gems left to see. This is the home stretch, so slow down, take that detour, and savor every last bit of this epic Route 66 journey before you hit the END OF THE TRAIL sign on Santa Monica Pier.

SANTA MONICA

66

End of the Trail

CREATIVE
EDGE
art & gifts

Leg 6:
Flagstaff to
Santa Monica

506 Miles

Find a **complete** Online Trip Guide
for leg 6:

rt.guide/NULR

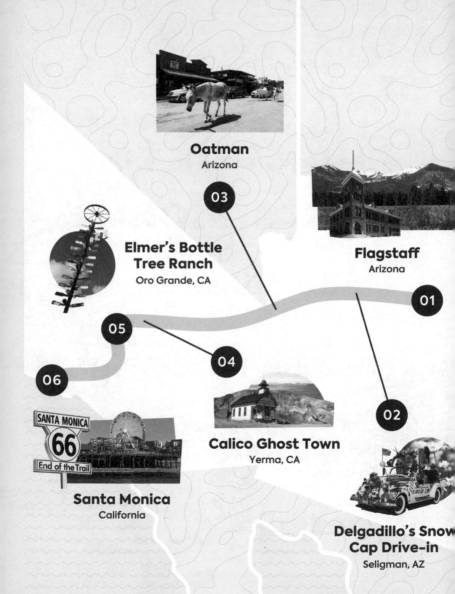

Oatman
Arizona

03

Elmer's Bottle Tree Ranch
Oro Grande, CA

Flagstaff
Arizona

01

05

04

06

02

SANTA MONICA
66
End of the Trail

Calico Ghost Town
Yerma, CA

Santa Monica
California

Delgadillo's Snow Cap Drive-in
Seligman, AZ

Leg 6:
Flagstaff to Santa Monica

Route highlights

01 Flagstaff

Delgadillo's Snow Cap Drive-In **02**

03 Oatman

Calico Ghost Town **04**

05 Elmer's Bottle Tree Ranch

Santa Monica **06**

Featured campgrounds

Grand Canyon Railway RV Park
601 W. Franklin Ave., Williams, AZ

This is a good place to camp for the night if you are looking to explore the Grand Canyon during your Route 66 adventure. It's only two blocks away from the route and downtown Williams. Take the Grand Canyon Railway into the national park and save yourself the drive.

Malibu Creek State Park Campground
1925 Las Virgenes Road, Calabasas, CA

Once you've reached the end of Route 66 in Santa Monica, head 20 miles northwest and camp in this scenic state park with beautiful views of Las Virgenes Valley and Malibu Canyon. Sites are available for trailers and motorhomes up to 30 feet long.

Featured accommodation

Wigwam Village No. 7 Motel
2728 W. Foothill Blvd., Rialto, CA

This is your last chance to sleep in an iconic Wigwam Village motel along Route 66, so don't pass it up. No. 7 was built by Frank Redford, creator of the motels. (Also see page 285.)

Playlist
Listen here: rt.guide/FLGJ

Songs to get you in the mood while on the road . . .

1. "Santa Monica," Everclear
2. "California," Joni Mitchell
3. "Seligman, Arizona," Ibrahim Maalouf
4. "Flagstaff," Evet + Ted
5. "Ghost Town," The Specials
6. "West Coast," Lana Del Rey
7. "Good Vibrations," The Beach Boys
8. "Surfin' USA," The Beach Boys
9. "L.A. Woman," The Doors
10. "Hotel California," the Eagles

On the road . . .
Arizona

This last stretch of the Mother Road—from western Arizona to the coast of California—is pretty lengthy, but there are plenty of detours and attractions to break up the drive.

On the road . . .
Flagstaff

Surrounded by national forests and designated wilderness areas, and just 80 miles south of the Grand Canyon, Flagstaff is an oasis of natural beauty with all the comforts and conveniences of a big city. Home to Northern Arizona University, it somehow manages to be a bustling college town with a quaint, small-town vibe. Its historic downtown is home to breweries, restaurants, and shops in buildings from the 1890s. Unlike the dry, sweltering desert cities in southern Arizona, Flagstaff—thanks to its elevation of nearly 7,000 feet—has a more comfortable four-season climate with plenty of snow in the winter, so plan accordingly.

Walnut Canyon National Monument
3 Walnut Canyon Road, Flagstaff, AZ

Walnut Canyon National Monument is a geological wonder. It was established in 1915 to protect ancient cliff dwellings, and the National Park Service took over the 3,600 acres in 1934. Step inside curved canyons, ascend towering cliffs, or hike the Rim and

OPPOSITE Walnut Canyon National Monument   *Traveller70/Shutterstock*

Island Trails. Remember to wear decent walking shoes and bring plenty of water.

Eden Pueblo
US 89 N., Flagstaff, AZ

Eden Pueblo, a fascinating and quick stop in north Flagstaff, was once the site of a Native American village. Located at the foot of Mount Eldon, it is believed to have been a part of a large-scale trade route for the Pueblo peoples.

Woody Mountain Campground
2727 W. Route 66, Flagstaff, AZ

Woody Mountain Campground is a family-owned and -operated campground nestled into a gorgeous and peaceful pine forest. The campground is a 40-minute drive from Meteor Crater and features an old-fashioned general store.

ABOVE Lobby of the Monte Vista Hotel
Bill Morrow/Flickr/CC BY 2.0 (creativecommons.org/licenses/by/2.0)

Weirdville

The haunted Hotel Monte Vista
100 N. San Francisco St., Flagstaff, AZ

The Hotel Monte Vista in Flagstaff has a rich history of famous guests, including Bing Crosby, Gary Cooper, and John Wayne. It also might be the most haunted hotel along Route 66. Wayne was one of the first people to suspect that the Monte Vista might have a bit of a ghost problem. He reported seeing the figure of a bellboy—but don't worry, Wayne claimed he was friendly. In 1970, the hotel allegedly picked up yet another ghost when a wounded bank robber died at the bar in the lounge. There have been more ghost sightings throughout the years, including a lady in a rocking chair and a crying baby in the basement.

ABOVE Lowell Observatory at night
Dominic Jeanmaire/Shutterstock

Diablo Burger
120 N. Leroux St., Flagstaff, AZ

Grab dinner at Diablo Burger if you're craving fresh food. The burgers are all made with open-range, antibiotic-free beef raised on local ranches.

Lowell Observatory
1400 W. Mars Hill Road, Flagstaff, AZ

The Lowell Observatory is considered one of the most important astronomical observatories in the world. Designated a National Landmark in 1965, the observatory's historic telescope is now available for public educational use. Head to the Steele Visitor Center to take a guided tour. Tours are available day or night, but the best time to visit is after dark, when the big telescope is set up along with several smaller ones. Regardless of the time, plan on spending at least a few hours here.

Starlight Pines Bed and Breakfast
3380 E. Lockett Road, Flagstaff, AZ

Flagstaff is a great place to spend the night. Starlight Pines Bed and Breakfast—with its claw-foot tubs, private balconies, delicious breakfasts, and comfy beds—will make you feel like royalty. Located just 10 minutes from downtown, this bed-and-breakfast has only four guest rooms, so be sure to book in advance.

 Extra stops

Miz Zip's *Restaurant*
2924 E. Route 66, Flagstaff, AZ

Route 66 Roadhouse *Restaurant*
11840 W. Route 66, Bellemont, AZ

On the road . . .
Williams

Williams was the final Route 66 town bypassed by I-40. The town took its battle against the bypass to the courts but stopped fighting in 1984. Despite the setbacks, Williams has held on thanks to its status as the Gateway to the Grand Canyon. This stretch of the Mother Road is particularly well preserved and features many eateries, shops, museums, parks, and lakes. Williams' Main Street has been designated a National Historic District, and it's a great place to relax and refuel before you tackle the Grand Canyon.

Rod's Steak House
301 E. Route 66, Williams, AZ

Grab a bite to eat at Rod's Steak House, known for its homemade rolls, steaks, and desserts. Located about an hour from Grand Canyon National Park, Rod's has been a Route 66 icon since 1946.

The Grand Canyon Railway
233 N. Grand Canyon Blvd., Williams, AZ

The Grand Canyon Railway was established in 1901. Jump on board to enjoy champagne, live entertainment, and gorgeous views.

ABOVE Route 66 in Williams, Arizona
MARCEL DE LIMA/Shutterstock

Extra stops

The Canyon Motel & RV Park *Accommodation*
1900 E. Rodeo Road, Williams, AZ

Twisters *Restaurant*
US 66, Williams, AZ

Goldie's Route 66 Diner *Restaurant*
425 E. US 66, Williams, AZ

Drover's Inn *Accommodation*
321 E. US 66, Williams, AZ

Grand Motel *Accommodation*
234 E. US 66, Williams, AZ

**Rodeway Inn & Suites Downtowner
Route 66** *Accommodation*
201E E. US 66, Williams, AZ

The Lodge on Route 66 *Accommodation*
200 E. US 66, Williams, AZ

Red Garter Inn *Accommodation*
137 W. Railroad Ave., Williams, AZ

Route 66 is divided into two separate east–west roads as it runs through Williams, so you'll have to drive through the town, then turn around and drive back in order to see all the iconic landmarks.

DETOUR

Grand Canyon National Park

20 S. Entrance Road, Grand Canyon, AZ

Words (and even pictures) simply cannot do Grand Canyon National Park justice—it's one of those truly epic places you just have to see in person to believe. Officially designated as a national park in 1919, the Grand Canyon sees more than 5 million visitors annually. The massive canyon was formed by erosion from the Colorado River after the plateau was lifted due to seismic activity, revealing rock that's more than a billion years old. Whether you take in the sweeping views from the top or hike into its depths, you'll quickly discover why it's one of the most iconic national parks in the U.S.

ABOVE View from Grandview Point
ToskanaINC/Shutterstock

Tips for Visiting the Grand Canyon

1. *Don't just snap a photo and call it a day.* Take the time to visit a few scenic viewpoints or, better yet, take a hike. The South Kaibab, Rim, and Grandview Trails all offer short routes and stunning views.

2. *Park your car.* The Grand Canyon has reliable public transportation and a shuttle service, both of which will help you save gas and keep you moving.

3. *Plan ahead.* The park is a popular destination year-round. Make reservations and book tours as far in advance as possible. Cancellations do happen, so if you prefer to fly by the seat of your pants, keep in mind that the best time to check for last-minute openings is a few days in advance of your trip.

4. *Prepare for the weather.* Spring and summer are the busiest times to visit the Grand Canyon, and summer means often-intense heat and afternoon thunderstorms. The North Rim closes in the winter—it occasionally snows—but crowds thin out a bit. Fall is also a great time to visit, when the temperatures start to cool off, even though it might still be crowded.

North Rim of Grand Canyon

Generally less crowded than the South Rim, the North Rim features a nice visitor center and

Our love letter to Grand Canyon National Park, in honor of its 100th birthday: **rt.guide/XXGB**

the Bright Angel Trailhead, which is less than a mile out and back. It takes you to the gorgeous Bright Angel Point, which offers panoramic views of the canyon. There are several other hikes and overlooks to be found on this side of the canyon as well, so schedule plenty of time to explore.

South Rim of Grand Canyon

The South Rim is the most popular place in the entire park, thanks to its accessibility, amenities, and epic views. It can get really crowded—particularly during sunrise and sunset—but it's worth fighting the crowds to see the canyon lit up in spectacular technicolor.

Desert View Watchtower

Part of what makes the Desert View Watchtower so cool is the crumbling base and haphazard-looking windows, but it was intentionally designed to look that way. No detail was left unnoticed by early 20th-century architect Mary Colter (one of the few female architects of her time). Colter designed several buildings in Grand Canyon National Park, including Hermit's Rest Snack Bar and Bright Angel Lodge. All of her designs combine traditional Southwest architectural styles with rustic and Native American elements.

The interior of the Desert View Watchtower is incredibly detailed, with multiple staircases and varied levels that allow you to see all the way to the top from the bottom floor. The win-

DETOUR

dows have reflectoscopes, which enhance the colors and tones of the landscapes.

The first floor of the tower, known as the kiva room, features a gift shop, and the observation deck, located at the top of the tower, offers stunning views of the eastern part of the South Rim.

Moran Point

The colorful view from Moran Point on the South Rim is popular for a reason: Here you can really sense the vastness of the canyon.

Grandview Point

Grandview Point, the southernmost point in the canyon, is the farthest from the river, so

ABOVE Moran Point at sunset
Tommy Larey/Shutterstock

the views here are a little more unique. Hike a short way down the Grandview Trail for even better, unobstructed views.

Yavapai Point

Yavapai Point, the lookout farthest north on the South Rim and closest to the Colorado River, offers yet another viewpoint. It's a quick walk west from Mather Point, although parking here is a little more limited.

Havasu Falls

The famously beautiful Havasu waterfalls are located on tribal land within the canyon and just outside the national park. If you're up for a multiday hike, it's well worth the trip. Just make sure to start planning early as hiking permits are both expensive and extremely difficult to get your hands on; reservations go on sale once a year and tend to sell out almost immediately.

BELOW Havasu Falls
Tampa Adventure Group/Shutterstock

DETOUR

Thinking of visiting Havasu Falls? Read our guide first: **rt.guide/SXYX**

Elves Chasm

Elves Chasm, possibly the best-kept secret in the park, is a magical grotto reachable only via a guided tour that includes hiking and rafting down the Colorado River.

Arizona Steakhouse

Many of the dining options in the Grand Canyon are notorious for being expensive and rather mediocre, but the Arizona Room is a solid choice for lunch or dinner. The steakhouse-esque menu features Southwest staples such as prickly pear, agave, green chile, native squash, bison, and cornmeal.

Pine Country Restaurant

The adorable Pine Country Restaurant is old school through and through, from the menu of classic favorites (think chicken and steak dinners) to the gift shop and incredibly warm service. Don't forget to save room for pie.

Red Raven Restaurant

It's nice to leave the park's lodge dining rooms and find some local gems. Red Raven is a great option for lunch or dinner if you're craving something funkier. It offers dishes that are a little more exciting than some of the other park options, such as ginger beef salad, brochette of lamb, and fruit and cheese plates.

Canyon Star Steakhouse and Saloon

Whether all that hiking has you craving a big steak dinner or you just want to unwind with a beer at the bar, the Canyon Star Steakhouse and Saloon has you covered. As a bonus, the stools in the saloon are made from authentic mule-runner saddles.

Extra stops

Ranch House Cafe *Restaurant*
83 W. Park Ave., Ash Fork, AZ

Oasis Lounge *Restaurant*
346 Park Ave., Ash Fork, AZ

Ash Fork Route 66 Museum *Attraction*
901 Old Route 66, Ash Fork, AZ

BELOW Crookton Overpass Bridge on Old Route 66 between Seligman and Ash Fork, Arizona *James McCray/Shutterstock*

DETOUR

On the road . . .
Seligman

Located in the heart of the northern Arizona high desert, Seligman occupies a very cozy enclave surrounded by mountains to the east, desert to the west, and the Grand Canyon to the north. Seligman's Main Street is lined with historic, locally owned businesses that, against all odds, have withstood the test of time.

Originally founded as a railroad town, Seligman was named after a railroad financier in 1886. With the establishment of Route 66 in 1926, Seligman became a popular stop for cross-country roadtrippers. I-40 bypassed the town in 1978, threatening businesses, but a local group successfully lobbied Arizona to designate Route 66 as a Historic Highway in 1987. Seligman's Chamber of Commerce began promoting the town as the Birthplace of Historic Route 66, and the town's historic district was listed on the National Register of Historic Places in 2005.

Seligman Historic District
Seligman, AZ

An inspiration for Disney's *Cars*, Seligman has retained its historical charm, working hard to preserve the early 20th-century buildings that line Main Street, Railroad Avenue, and Chino Street. Throughout town you'll see old-timey cars parked in front of businesses, which make for great photo ops.

Stagecoach 66 Motel
21455 I-40 Business Loop, Exit 123,
  Seligman, AZ

The largest motel in Seligman is the Stagecoach 66 Motel. It has some great neon out front; a few themed rooms (including one inspired by *Cars*); an on-site pizza joint with a bar and pool table; WiFi; and coffee and pastries in the morning. Even if you don't stay the night, snap a picture with the sign and chat up locals in the bar over a cold beer.

Route 66 RoadRunner
22330 W. Old Highway 66, Seligman, AZ

The Route 66 RoadRunner is located in the old Olsen's Chevrolet dealership and garage building. Built in 1936, it features a classic adobe look and original redwood beams. The souvenir shop sells the expected Route 66 kitsch, along with locally crafted Native American jewelry. The restaurant serves up snacks and to-go grub such as ice cream, coffee, and breakfast burritos, plus sandwiches, burgers, hot dogs, and booze.

The Black Cat Bar
114 W. Chino St., Seligman, AZ

The Black Cat Bar has existed in some form since the early 1900s, keeping locals liquored up and happy. Today, it remains a no-frills, cash-only, down-to-earth joint where you can enjoy a stiff drink with locals. Play pool or just enjoy a drink on the patio before retiring to your motel for the evening. This place is true-blue Seligman to the core.

Historic Seligman Sundries
22405 Historic Route 66, Seligman, AZ

The Historic Seligman Sundries is located in one of the town's oldest buildings, which dates back to 1904. It's utterly adorable and has been a dance hall, a theater, a trading post, and a soda fountain. It was refurbished in 2005, and a lot of the signs hanging up inside are authentic vintage artifacts uncovered during the renovations. Sit at the counter, which used to serve as a soda fountain, and enjoy a coffee or bottled soda.

Historic Route 66 Motel
22750 AZ 66 Scenic, Seligman, AZ

The Historic Route 66 Motel is a small, authentic motor lodge that maintains an old-school charm while offering modern amenities.

Roadkill Cafe
22830 AZ 66, Seligman, AZ

The Roadkill Cafe sets itself apart from other retro diners on the route by being totally strange. The menu features dishes such as Bad-Brake Steak, Fender Tenders, Splatter Platter, Swirl of Squirrel, and Highway Hash. The same building houses the O.K. Saloon, which features Wild West memorabilia and pays tribute to Arizona's rough-and-tumble past.

The Rusty Bolt
22345 W. Old Highway 66, Seligman, AZ

As far as photo ops in Seligman go, The Rusty Bolt is easily the most ridiculous. Old storefronts are lined with signs and topped with mannequins in wacky costumes. Humorous jokes, weird props, eccentric employees, and cute souvenirs make this a must-stop.

BELOW You'll find plenty of weird photo props at The Rusty Bolt.

Delgadillo's Snow Cap Drive-In

SPOTLIGHT

22235 Historic Route 66, Seligman, AZ

When Juan and Mary Delgadillo opened the Snow Cap Drive-In on Route 66 in Seligman in 1953, they probably didn't anticipate it becoming a worldwide tourist attraction. More than 60 years later, Delgadillo's Snow Cap Drive-In is one of the most sought-out Route 66 destinations. Built with scrap lumber from the Santa Fe railroad yard, the Delgadillo family constructed the drive-in on an absolute shoestring budget.

To attract travelers, Juan took a 1936 Chevy, cut the top off, and decorated it with every weird paint color and doodad he could find, including a Christmas tree in the back. The plan worked, and it's still one of the most photographed pieces of Route 66 Americana.

Known for bantering back and forth with his customers, Juan would often joke, "Do you want cheese on that cheeseburger?" He passed away in 2004, but his spirit lives on at the Snow Cap today.

The drive-in isn't the only iconic Route 66 location in the Delgadillo family. Juan's brother, Angel, made his mark on the Mother Road with his barber shop (now a gift store). Angel, affectionately known as the guardian angel of Route 66, founded the Historic Route 66 Association of Arizona in 1987, a move that would quickly be imitated in other states along the route.

Angel and Juan are regarded in such high esteem that when Pixar's John Lasseter wanted to learn more about Route 66 for his movie *Cars,* he went to Angel for a history lesson. The friendly barber told the tragic tale of how traffic all but dried up after I-40 opened. Both brothers are listed in the credits of *Cars,* and if you stop by Angel's Barbershop, you'll see a signed *Toy Story* sketch hanging on the wall.

ABOVE Hackberry General Store
Ralph Resch/Shutterstock

Hackberry General Store
11255 E. AZ 66, Hackberry, AZ

Hackberry General Store is a travel photographer's playground. You may not find gas here, but you will find vintage gas pumps, beautiful signage, a diner, and rusty cars to photograph to your heart's content.

Extra stops

Antares Curve *Attraction*
W. Historic Route 66, Antares, AZ

Giganticus Headicus/Antares Visitor Center
Attraction 9855 AZ 66, Kingman, AZ

On the road...
Kingman

Kingman sits at the heart of an unbroken, 158-mile stretch of the Mother Road. Its historic downtown includes museums, historic homes, hiking trails, colorful murals, and more than 40 places listed on the National Register of Historic Places.

Mike's Route 66 Outpost & Saloon
9321 E. AZ 66, Kingman, AZ

Mike's Route 66 Outpost & Saloon is beloved by locals and tourists alike, but it's not just a dive bar and pub—it's also an RV park where you can enjoy a cold beer after a long drive and tuck in for the night. The Outpost is situated right next to the train tracks, so be prepared for trains to pass by every 15 minutes or so.

Hualapai Mountain Resort
4525 Hualapai Mountain Road, Kingman, AZ

Nestled between towering pines, just 13 miles southeast of Kingman, you'll find the Hualapai Mountain Resort, a popular destination for mountain weddings, honeymoons, and romantic weekend escapes. If you love hiking, camping, cycling, or picnics with a view, this place rocks.

Mr D'z Route 66 Diner
105 E. Andy Devine Ave., Kingman, AZ

Another classic Arizona road-food stop is Mr D'z Route 66 Diner. The retro diner prides itself on its home-cooked food and family-friendly vibe. Try the chicken-fried steak and wash it down with a root beer float.

Extra stops

El Trovatore Motel *Accommodation*
1440 E. Andy Devine Ave., Kingman, AZ

Hotel Brunswick *Accommodation*
315 E. Andy Devine Ave., Kingman, AZ

Powerhouse Visitor Center *Attraction*
120 W. Andy Devine Ave., #2, Kingman, AZ

Locomotive Park *Attraction*
310 W. Beale St., Kingman, AZ

Mohave Museum of History and Arts *Attraction*
400 W. Beale St., Kingman, AZ

Colin Michael Baker/Shutterstock

ABOVE Steam locomotive on display in Kingman's Locomotive Park

Clark Gable and Carole Lombard got married at a Methodist church in Kingman, Arizona.

DETOUR

A town called Nothing

This Arizona ghost town lives up to its name in more ways than one. It's in the middle of nowhere, there's no fascinating story behind how it got its name, and there's not much to see or do. But that hasn't always been the case.

Back when Nothing was founded in the late 1970s, it had a gas station and garage. Despite the remote location, the gas station operated until 2005, when it was sold. The new owner took out the gas pumps, fenced it off, and put it up for sale again. The third owner planned to revive Nothing with a restaurant but had a hard time implementing his plan to open an eatery in the middle of nowhere.

So now Nothing is back to being, well, nothing. There's one boarded-up, abandoned building and signs declaring that you're in Nothing, which make for good photo ops.

Above: Straight 8 Photography/Shutterstock

Cool Springs Gas Station

Old Route 66, Golden Valley, AZ

While on your way to or from Oatman, stop at this Route 66 icon. Dating back to the 1920s, it was once one of only a few places to fill up on the Arizona portion of the route. Right before the intense drive through the Black Mountains, with its steep grades and hairpin curves, Cool Springs was the ideal place to grab some food. As the road's popularity waned in favor of the interstate, the business began to struggle, and after a fire in the 1960s, it was left abandoned.

Other than a brief appearance in the 1991 Jean-Claude Van Damme movie *Universal Soldier*, the filling station was mostly forgotten until 1997, when it caught the eye of a man named Ned Leuchtner as he traveled along Route 66. Leuchtner bought the property in 2001 and reopened it in 2004. Today, it's a small museum, gift shop, and photo op.

On the road . . .
Oatman

You'd be hard-pressed to find a ghost town more real—
or more alive—than Oatman. Located at the edge of
Arizona on Route 66 and perched 2,700 feet above sea
level in the Black Mountains, Oatman is a strange place
run by wild burros.

In 1908, gold was discovered in the Black Mountains, and many prospectors flocked to Oatman to stake
their claims. For the remainder of the 19th century,
mining in the area steadily decreased, and in 1921, a fire
ripped through town, destroying most of the buildings.
I-40 bypassed Oatman in the early 1950s, and nearly a
decade later, it was a virtual ghost town.

But the people of Oatman fought to survive, and
now the town has more than 40 shops, eateries, and
other attractions, including Wild West reenactments,
gunslinging shows, annual bed races, a sidewalk egg-
fry contest, Gold Camp Days, the International Burro
Bisket Toss, and a yearly book fair and bake sale.

 Lured by gold, ghosts, and roaming burros,
visitors just can't quit the tiny mountain town
of Oatman, Arizona. Here's why: **rt.guide/ZFVN**

The Glory Hole
1 Main St., Oatman, AZ

The Glory Hole, famously featured in the 1962 Western *How the West Was Won*, is an antiques and collect-
ibles store located in a historic building.

Olive Oatman Restaurant & Saloon
170 Route 66, Oatman, AZ

Like the town itself, the casual Olive Oatman Restaurant is named for a young woman from Illinois who was reportedly kidnapped by the Yavapai tribe on a trip out West. Try the Navajo fry bread (served savory or with ice cream and fruit), play a tune on the player piano, or cool off with a root beer float and air conditioning.

Oatman Hotel and Dollar Bill Bar
181 Main St., Oatman, AZ

Built in 1902, just before the final major gold rush, the two-story adobe hotel is a famous landmark. It was rebuilt after the 1921 fire. In 1939, Clark Gable and Carole Lombard checked in for their honeymoon. Gable returned often to play poker, and visitors still claim to hear the two lovebirds whispering and laughing from the room where they stayed. The spirit of an Irish miner, nicknamed Oatie, who died behind the hotel, supposedly also roams the halls playing the bagpipes.

Tourists have been signing singles and hanging them on the walls and ceiling of the Dollar Bill Bar for ages. The tradition reportedly started back in the town's mining days, when miners would take a dollar from their check on payday, write their name on it, and hang it up on the bar's wall as a tab that they could use until they got paid again.

Judy's Saloon
260 Oatman-Topock Highway, Oatman, AZ

If you're looking to hang out with locals or happen to be rolling into town after 5 p.m., Judy's Saloon is your best bet. The beer is cold, the iced tea is sweet, the crowd is awesome, the music is rocking, and the manager is said to be the "rudest bartender on Route 66" (their words, not ours).

DETOUR

Nevada

Although the route never technically passes through Nevada, you'll be close enough to take a detour on your way from Kingman, Arizona, to Needles, California.

Grapevine Canyon
Grapevine Canyon Road, Laughlin, NV

Grapevine Canyon is home to ancient petroglyphs and a natural spring. Located in the Bridge Canyon Wilderness Area, it's a gorgeous place to wander around and explore. The trail to the freshwater spring is a strenuous hike, and temperatures in the area can reach 120°F during summer, so bring water, sunscreen, and proper hiking shoes. Don't touch the petroglyphs, but feel free to take photos and admire them from a distance.

Pioneer Saloon
310 W. Spring St., Goodsprings, NV

Pioneer Saloon, less than 20 minutes from the freeway, looks straight out of a postapocalyptic movie. The saloon's parlor room features historical newspaper clippings, and the General Store is stocked with tchotchkes and souvenirs.

ABOVE Petroglyphs in Grapevine Canyon *Felipe Sanchez/Shutterstock*

On the road . . . California

The California section of Route 66 will give you a proper taste of the Golden State's diverse scenery, from tiny desert ghost towns to the urban sprawl of Los Angeles. This stretch is also packed with iconic roadside attractions. Take your time and meander through the glass forest at Elmer's Bottle Tree Ranch, or get your photo taken next to the freshly restored neon sign at Roy's Motel and Cafe. Before you know it, you'll be finishing this epic journey at the end of the Santa Monica Pier, where the West Coast meets the Pacific Ocean.

El Garces
950 Front St., Needles, CA

Before Route 66, travelers primarily headed west by train. In 1908, the El Garces opened in Needles, providing a stop for rail passengers. The Classical Revival–style depot included a hotel and Harvey House restaurant; it was the height of luxury, unusual for a town as small as Needles. In 1949, as Route 66 was at its peak, El Garces closed its Harvey House, and the railroad used it as offices through the 1980s. The city purchased the building in 1999, and it was placed on the National Register of Historic Places in 2002. After extensive renovations, El Garces is now open for guided tours.

ABOVE Needles, California, welcomes you.
Matthew Thomas Allen/Shutterstock

Extra stops

Fender's River Road Resort *Accommodation*
3396 Needles Highway, Needles, CA

Goffs Schoolhouse *Attraction*
37198 Lanfair Road, Essex, CA

Zzyzx
Baker, CA

Zzyzx (formerly known as Soda Springs) is located at the end of Zzyzx Road, a 4.3-mile-long rural road off I-15. Once the site of a health resort, it's now home to California State University's Desert Studies Center. This strange oasis is worth a visit, and not just for its bizarre name (pronounced zye-zix).

BELOW Man-made Lake Tuendae at the Desert Studies Center in Zzyzx
Mariusz S. Jurgielewicz/Shutterstock

Ludlow Cafe
68315 National Trails Highway, Ludlow, CA

The historic Ludlow Cafe is renowned for its home-cooked food. Housed in a charming A-frame building, the café is conveniently located across the street from a gas station and next door to a hotel.

Roy's Motel and Cafe
87520 National Trails Highway, Amboy, CA

Roy's is located along a desolate stretch of the Mother Road in the tiny desert town of Amboy. The motel, café, and gas station has appeared in numerous movies and is one of the best photo ops along the entire route. The iconic neon sign has recently been restored, so it looks great day or night.

Amboy Crater
16700 Crater Road, Amboy, CA

Amboy Crater, a 250-foot-tall symmetrical volcanic cinder cone, was designated a National Natural Landmark in 1973. Its 24 square miles of lava flows surround the crater, and you can hike by lava lakes, basalt flows, and collapsed lava tubes.

OPPOSITE Roy's Motel and Cafe's recently restored neon sign
Stephanie Puglisi

ROY'S

VACANCY

MOTEL
CAFE

ROUTE
US
66

ABOVE Amboy Crater
Kris Clifford/Shutterstock

The ups and downs of Amboy, a town so tiny
that if you blink, you might miss it: **rt.guide/AAJE**

Bagdad Cafe
46548 National Trails Highway,
  Newberry Springs, CA

Although it's a Route 66 icon, the Bagdad Cafe is
actually the second incarnation of the original café,
which was located in Bagdad, a town between
Amboy and Ludlow. The Newberry Springs café
was renamed Bagdad Cafe when a Route 66 film
was shot in the area. Filming wrapped, but the
name stayed.

Peggy Sue's '50s Diner
35654 Yermo Road, Yermo, CA

Built in 1954, Peggy Sue's is set against the dramatic
backdrop of the Calico Mountains. The ambience will
make you feel as if you've just stepped into an episode of *Happy Days*, and the portions are generous.

Calico Ghost Town
36600 Ghost Town Road, Yermo, CA

If Oatman and its wild burros were a bit too rowdy for your taste, Calico Ghost Town might be a better bet. It's a bit touristy and maintained by the regional park system, but it has a nice campground and several old buildings to explore, including museums, shops, and restaurants.

Extra stops

Daggett Garage *Attraction*
35565 Santa Fe St., Daggett, CA

Desert Market *Shop*
35596 Santa Fe Ave., Daggett, CA

Barstow Station
1611 E. Main St., Barstow, CA

Barstow Station is a reliable pit stop for food and people-watching. The fourth-largest seller of lottery tickets in California is also a good place to stock up on booze or last-minute souvenirs.

Route 66 Mother Road Museum
681 N. First Ave., Barstow, CA

Established in 2000, the Route 66 Mother Road Museum is one of the final museums on the route dedicated to its history. Housed in the historic Casa del Desierto Harvey House, the building makes for a great photo.

Western America Railroad Museum
685 N. First Ave., Barstow, CA

The Western American Railroad Museum showcases outdoor displays, locomotives, and other huge pieces of railroad machinery.

Extra stops

Casa del Desierto (Barstow Harvey House)
Attraction 685 N. First Ave., Barstow, CA

El Rancho Hotel *Accommodation*
112 E. Main St., Barstow, CA

Route 66 Motel *Accommodation*
195 W. Main St., Barstow, CA

Helendale Market *Shop*
26428 National Trails Highway, Helendale, CA

Sage Brush Inn Gas Station *Attraction*
24763 National Trails Highway, Oro Grande, CA

Antique Station *Shop*
19176 National Trails Highway, Oro Grande, CA

Emma Jean's Holland Burger Cafe *Restaurant*
17143 N. D St., Victorville, CA

California Route 66 Museum *Attraction*
16825 S. D St., Victorville, CA

The Outpost Cafe *Restaurant*
8685 US 395, Oak Hills, CA

Elmer's Bottle Tree Ranch
24266 National Trails Highway,
Oro Grande, CA

At Elmer's Bottle Tree Ranch, you'll find about 200 "trees" made of colorful bottles. The found art displays shimmer in the sun alongside bird feeders, road signs, gas pumps, bicycles, and cars.

 Elmer's Bottle Tree Ranch is more than a roadside attraction; it's a shrine to a father and son's relationship: **rt.guide/NJNH**

BELOW Elmer's Bottle Tree Ranch
Mr.C/Shutterstock

First Original McDonald's Museum
1398 N. E St., San Bernardino, CA

This is the original McDonald's location, owned and operated by the McDonald brothers (the first franchised location opened by Ray Kroc was located in Des Plaines, Illinois). The brothers forever changed the restaurant industry by firing the car hops, cutting the menu down to the most popular items, and optimizing their successful diner for efficiency, consistency, and value. Even if you're not a fan of the Golden Arches, you have to respect how much they revolutionized the fast-food industry—for better or worse. The museum is full of memorabilia, but we're especially fond of pieces from the McDonaldLand era.

BELOW The site of the first McDonald's location, now a museum
Tripp/Flickr/CC BY 2.0 (creativecommons.org/licenses/by/2.0)

Wigwam Village Motel No. 7

SPOTLIGHT

2728 W. Foothill Blvd., Rialto, CA

You don't want to miss your last opportunity to "sleepee in a teepee" on the Mother Road. Once scattered across the country, today only three Wigwam Villages remain.

The Patels, owners of No. 7, live and breathe Route 66 and do an exceptional job promoting and encouraging its preservation. This is a great place to stay with kids, and it's the only Wigwam Village that still has its original kidney-shaped pool. Everything you look for in a motel is available here in a whimsical package—each individual teepee includes a refrigerator, a bathroom with a shower, a cozy bed, and an air conditioner.

Built in 1949, the California Wigwam Motel is technically located within the city limits of San Bernardino, although it has a Rialto postal address. It was the last of the Wigwam Motels to be built, and, thanks to the Patels, its rooms are clean and lovingly maintained.

Mitla Cafe
602 N. Mt. Vernon Ave., San Bernardino, CA

For more than 75 years, this charming café has been serving amazing Mexican food. It was one of the first Mexican restaurants in the U.S., and legend says this place inspired the founders of Taco Bell.

Cucamonga Service Station
9670 Foothill Blvd., Rancho Cucamonga, CA

The Cucamonga Service Station, constructed in 1915, actually predates Route 66. From 1925 until 1944, it operated as a Richfield Oil Service Station; today it's owned by local nonprofit Route 66 Inland Empire California (IECA) and houses a gift shop and museum.

Aztec Hotel
311 W. Foothill Blvd., Monrovia, CA

Monrovia's Aztec Hotel was built in 1925 and remains a curiosity to this day for its distinctive Mayan architectural style. The Aztec, which was located along Route 66 until a 1931 realignment took the official route away from the hotel, was placed on the National Register of Historic Places in 1978.

Fair Oaks Pharmacy
1526 Mission St., South Pasadena, CA

A California institution since 1915, the Fair Oaks Pharmacy underwent a restoration in the 1990s and still functions as a real pharmacy, if you need a prescription filled before heading out on the road. The real draw, however, is the soda fountain where soda jerks serve old-fashioned phosphates, lime rickeys, and egg creams in addition to hot dogs, hamburgers, sandwiches, and salads.

Extra stops

Sycamore Inn Prime Steakhouse *Restaurant*
8318 Foothill Blvd., Rancho Cucamonga, CA

Magic Lamp Inn *Restaurant*
8189 Foothill Blvd., Rancho Cucamonga, CA

Madonna of the Trail *Attraction*
1010 Euclid Ave., Upland, CA

Wolfe's Market *Restaurant*
160 W. Foothill Blvd., Claremont, CA

Pinnacle Peak Steakhouse *Restaurant*
269 Foothill Blvd., San Dimas, CA

Saga Motor Hotel *Hotel*
1633 E. Colorado Blvd., Pasadena, CA

Andy's Coffee Shop *Restaurant*
1234 E. Colorado Blvd., Pasadena, CA

Rialto Theatre *Attraction*
1023 Fair Oaks Ave., South Pasadena, CA

On the road . . .
Santa Monica

You'll know you're at the end of your journey once you arrive at the Pacific Ocean. But to reach the official end-point of Route 66—and take a photo of the iconic END OF THE TRAIL sign—you'll have to ditch the car and walk to the end of the Santa Monica Pier. The coastal city of Santa Monica is also home to the original Muscle Beach outdoor gym and the pier's Pacific Park amusement park.

HI Los Angeles Santa Monica Hostel
1436 Second St., Santa Monica, CA

If you're traveling on a budget, Hostelling International is a great choice for spending the night. Located right near the beach, this airy hostel is the

BELOW Santa Monica Pier

perfect place to end your Route 66 adventure. The rooms are luxurious by hostel standards, and staying here will get you some special food and travel deals as well.

Santa Monica Pier
1614 Ocean Front Walk, Los Angeles, CA

Whether you call it the starting or ending point of the Mother Road, the Santa Monica Pier is the perfect spot to stretch your legs or snap photos of the ocean before embarking on a 2,000-mile trip east. Sure it's touristy, but that shouldn't stop you from taking a ride on the 1922 carousel or grabbing something sweet from the soda fountain. From the roller coaster and Ferris wheel to the arcade and the sign noting that it is the official end of Route 66, there's tons of fun to be had here.

48 Hours in Los Angeles

The beaches, warm weather, endless entertainment, celebrities, and rich history make LA one of the most popular destinations in the U.S. Enjoy the beautiful people and the effortlessly cool and laid-back culture of this famed SoCal city.

Hollywood Walk of Fame
6800 block of Hollywood Blvd.

Yes, it's touristy and kitschy, but you can't visit LA without at least driving down Hollywood Boulevard to see the stars on the Hollywood Walk of Fame. Whether you're searching for your favorite movie stars, putting your hands in their handprints at TCL Chinese Theatre Imax (inset), or you just want to get a good view of the HOLLYWOOD sign, this should be your first stop in the City of Angels.

Warner Brothers Studio Tour
3400 Warner Blvd., Burbank, CA

Since the film industry is such a massive part of LA, you might as well go behind the scenes. The Warner Brothers Studio Tour is fantastic, offering visitors a

ABOVE The Last Bookstore

glimpse of soundstages, props, cars, and more. You'll see a little bit of everything from iconic movies and TV shows such as *Batman*, *Friends*, and *Harry Potter*.

The Last Bookstore
453 S. Spring St., Los Angeles, CA

The Last Bookstore is proof that despite the glamour, LA can also get intellectual. Not only is this spacious store gorgeous, but it's also reasonably priced and filled to the brim with interesting titles both used and new. Don't miss the upstairs art gallery featuring a labyrinth made entirely out of books.

Go beyond the glitz and discover an unexpectedly whimsical side of Los Angeles:
rt.guide/YBHC

Trejo's Tacos
1556 N. Cahuenga Blvd., Los Angeles, CA

Throw a rock in any direction in Los Angeles and chances are you'll hit an authentic taco shop. For a celebrity-infused twist on the Mexican staple, hit up Trejo's Tacos. This local chain is owned by actor Danny Trejo, perhaps most famous for his titular role in *Machete*. Don't just take it from us—Anthony Bourdain called this place "really good."

Whisky a Go Go
8901 W. Sunset Blvd., West Hollywood, CA

Make sure you snag tickets in advance to this legendary nightclub, famous for hosting acts such as The Doors, Janis Joplin, and Led Zeppelin. It is credited with creating the go-go dancer fad of the late 1960s and still puts on shows for up-and-coming acts.

The Comedy Store
8433 Sunset Blvd., Los Angeles, CA

If you'd rather see something a little lighter, stop by The Comedy Store. Grab tickets to a show in one of three theaters offering all different kinds of performances, from big headlining acts to strange and offbeat smaller shows. There's a two-drink minimum here, but it doesn't have to be booze.

Good Times at Davey Wayne's
1611 N. El Centro Ave., Los Angeles, CA

End your night at Good Times at Davey Wayne's, a funky, 1970s-themed dive bar. Enter through an old refrigerator and step into a replica of what Hollywood looked like at its grooviest. The psychedelic music, strong drinks (try the boozy snow cones), and friendly crowd make this place a popular stop. Note that this establishment has a dress code: comfy, but no athletic wear or shorts and sandals after dark.

Chateau Marmont
8221 Sunset Blvd., Los Angeles, CA

Grab some breakfast at the famed (and allegedly haunted) French-inspired Chateau Marmont (inset), in the Hollywood Hills. Whether you're in the mood for decadent eggs Benedict or a cold-pressed juice, you can enjoy it in this old-school Hollywood hot spot. It's a good place for celebrity-spotting, but be discreet: The hotel will kick you out for gawking, taking photos, or approaching celebrities.

Conjuring up a ghost at Chateau Marmont, one of the most haunted hotels in Los Angeles: **rt.guide/LUBM**

Museum of Jurassic Technology
9341 Venice Blvd., Culver City, CA

Visiting the Museum of Jurassic Technology is a strange experience. Explore the dark, mysterious rooms and check out the bizarre exhibits. Don't miss the portrait gallery of Russian space dogs, the lovely tea room (with cookies), or the aviary.

Venice Beach Boardwalk
1800 Ocean Front Walk, Venice, CA

Everything you may have heard about the Venice Beach Boardwalk is probably true. Within seconds of stepping onto the boardwalk, you'll see fortune-tellers, folk artists, people doing yoga, and skateboarders in weird costumes. Wander around and soak in the strange and bizzare; check out the skate-dancing plaza, Muscle Beach, the basketball courts, and the freak show; or join a drum circle on the beach.

Venice Canal Historic District
Venice, CA

Developer Abbot Kinney built the canals in Venice in 1905, in an attempt to mimic the look and feel of their Italian namesake. But the rocketing popularity of the automobile made people change their tune on the once-scenic canals. Some were filled in for roads, while others fell into disrepair, and disputes over how to deal with them raged for years. In the 1990s, the Venice Canal Historic District was cleaned up and redeveloped, and today you can see some swanky homes here.

Time Travel Mart
12515 Venice Blvd., Los Angeles, CA

If the next stop on your road trip is the distant past or the near future, you'll need to stock up on supplies at the Time Travel Mart. Whether you need mad-scientist goggles, a "pastport," or a conquistador helmet, this quirky little store has all kinds of silly souvenirs. And the best part? The store is actually a front for a nonprofit dedicated to helping kids improve their writing skills, with all proceeds benefiting 826LA.

In 1936, Route 66 was extended from Los Angeles to Santa Monica, where the western terminus remains today.

Rustic Canyon
1119 Wilshire Blvd., Santa Monica, CA

Rustic Canyon is an upscale, casual wine bar and restaurant that's quintessential California. Everything on the menu, which changes daily, is creative and fresh. California is known for its wineries, so you won't find a better place to enjoy a glass or two with your dinner.

The Wellesbourne
10929 W. Pico Blvd., Los Angeles, CA

The Wellesbourne feels like the library of an eccentric rich person's mansion. Walls lined with books and English antiques somehow vibe perfectly with foosball and shuffleboard tables at this bar and lounge, which serves up modern takes on classic drinks.

How the Los Angeles portion of Route 66 is reaching a new generation of travelers: **rt.guide/RDYT**

Congratulations!

You have reached the end of the Mother Road—and by now you know it's not the destination that matters; it's the journey. But whether the Santa Monica Pier is your ending or starting point, take some time to celebrate and reflect. With more than 2,000 miles of classic neon, motels, larger-than-life roadside attractions, museums, diners, and countless colorful characters, the allure of Route 66 is as strong as ever. The road may look different today than it did decades ago—or even yesterday—but that's all part of the fun.

Photography credits

Index

Contributors

Tatiana Parent, Author

From New England to Old England, via Polynesia, Deutschland, and the Midwest, Tatiana has planted roots around the world and burned tons of rubber across the U.S. After receiving a doctorate in history, she developed an interest in the fading edges of a civilization a bit closer to home. She went on to co-found Roadtrippers and spent over a decade exploring America's highways and byways, incredible hidden gems, and roadside wonders.

Sanna Boman

Sanna is the lead editor of *Roadtrippers Magazine*. As an avid motorcycle rider, she's always planning her next two-wheeled road trip. Next on the bucket list? Visiting every national park in the U.S.

Alexandra Charitan

Alexandra is the managing editor of *Roadtrippers Magazine*. She likes things that are bigger or smaller than they should be: novelty architecture, miniature worlds, and anything made from fiberglass or neon. She dreams of visiting every state in the U.S. and will always stop for a Muffler Man.

Stephanie Puglisi

Stephanie Puglisi is the head of content at Roadtrippers. She is the co-author of *Idiot's Guides: RV Vacations* and *See You at the Campground: A Guide to Discovering Community, Connection, and a Happier Family in the Great Outdoors*. She roadtrips in the family RV with her husband, three sons, and sweet Maggie the camping dog.

Melissa Haskin

Melissa Haskin is a fact-checker and editor with over a decade of experience. She served as a fact-checker for the 2014, 2015, and 2016 editions of *The Unofficial Guide to Walt Disney World* and has fact-checked articles in publications such as *Men's Health* and *Cooking Light*. An eager traveler, Melissa is looking to visit her 39th state this summer: Montana.

Tag Christof

Tag Christof is an artist and writer who's lived at both ends and a couple of places along the middle of Route 66. His photo work and essays on architecture, American design, and the road have appeared in dozens of publications. Find him hiking the mean streets of Los Angeles or cruising his '79 Buick.

ABOVE Pere Marquette State Park in Grafton, Illinois (page 60)